One-Minute Devotions

God's best Secrets

ANDREW MURRAY

CHRISTIAN ART
Vereeniging

CHRIST CRUCIFIED

"God forbid that I should glory, save in the Cross of our Lord Jesus Christ, through which the world hath been crucified unto me, and I unto the world."
Gal. 6:14

It is the crucified Jesus who promises, who offers, to be with me every day. May not this be one reason why we find it so difficult to expect and enjoy the abiding presence? – because we do not glory in the Cross by which we are crucified to the world.

CHRIST GLORIFIED

"The Lamb which is in the midst of the throne shall be their shepherd."
"These are they which follow the Lamb whithersoever He goeth."
Rev. 7:17; 14:4

Oh, Christian, do believe that the Lamb in the midst of the throne is in very deed the embodiment of the omnipotent glory of the everlasting God and of His love; and that to have this Lamb of God as your almighty Shepherd and your faithful Keeper does indeed make it possible that the thoughts and the cares of earth shall indeed not prevail to separate you from His love for a single moment.

The Great Question

"Believe ye that I am able to do this? They said unto Him, Yea, Lord."
Mark 9:28

It is well that we understand clearly what the conditions are on which Christ offers to reveal to us in experience the secret of His abiding presence. God cannot force His blessings on us against our will. He seeks in every possible way to stir our desire and to help us to realize that He is able and most willing to make His promises true.

CHRIST MANIFESTING SELF

*"He that hath My commandments,
and keepeth them, he it is that
loveth Me: and he that loveth Me
shall be loved of My Father, and I
will love him, and will manifest
Myself unto him."*
John 14:21

The love of heaven shed abroad in the heart
would be met by the new and blessed revelation of Christ Himself. In the heart thus prepared by the Holy Spirit, showing itself in the obedience of love in a fully surrendered heart, the Father and the Son will take up their abode.

MARY: THE MORNING WATCH

"Jesus saith unto her; Mary! She turned herself, and saith unto Him, Rabboni! which is to say, Master."
John 20:16

There is nothing that can prove a greater attraction to our Lord than the love that sacrifices everything and rests satisfied with nothing less than Himself. It is to such a love that Christ manifests Himself. He loved us and gave Himself for us. Christ's love needs our love in which to reveal itself.

EMMAUS: THE EVENING PRAYER

"They constrained Him saying, Abide with us ... And He went in to tarry with them. And ... as He sat at meat with them ... their eyes were opened, and they knew Him."
Luke 24:29-31

What was it that led our Lord to reveal Himself to these two men? Nothing less than this, their intense devotion to their Lord. To such intense devotion and constraining prayer, the Lord's message will be given in power: "Lo, I am with you alway"; our eyes will be opened, and we will know Him and the blessed secret of the abiding presence always.

The Disciples: Their Divine Mission

"The same day at evening ... came Jesus and stood in the midst, and saith unto them, Peace be unto you."
John 20:19

Here He meets the willing servants whom He had trained for His service and hands over to them the work He had done on earth. He changes their fear into the boldness of peace and gladness. He ascends to the Father; the work the Father had given Him to do He now entrusts to them. The Divine Mission is now theirs to make known and carry out to victory.

Thomas: The Blessedness Of Believing

"... blessed are they that have not seen, and yet have believed."
John 20:29

Here, even now, after the lapse of all these centuries, we may have experienced the presence and power of Christ in a far deeper reality than Thomas did. To those who see not, yet believe, simply, only, truly, fully, believe in what Christ is and can be to them every moment, He has promised that He will manifest Himself and that the Father and He will come and dwell in them.

PETER: THE GREATNESS OF LOVE

"Peter was grieved because He said unto him the third time, Lovest thou Me? He said unto Him, Lord, Thou ... knowest that I love Thee."
John 21:17

To everyone who longs to have Jesus manifest Himself – "I am with you alway" – the essential requisite is love. Peter teaches us that such love is not in our power. But such love came to him through the power of Christ's death to sin and His resurrection life of which Peter became partaker. Thank God, if Peter the self-confident could be so changed, shall not we believe that Christ will work in us the wondrous change too.

JOHN: LIFE FROM THE DEAD

"And when I saw Him, I fell at His feet as one dead. And He laid His right hand upon me, saying, Fear not; I am the First and the Last, and the Living One; and I was dead, and behold, I am alive forevermore."
Rev. 1:17-18

Let us accept the lesson – through death to life. In the power of Christ Jesus with whom we have been crucified and whose death now works in us, if we will yield ourselves to it, death to sin, death to the world with all its self-pleasing and self-exaltation is to be the deepest law of our spiritual life.

PAUL: CHRIST REVEALED IN HIM

*"It was the good pleasure of God ...
to reveal His Son in Me."*
Gal. 1:15-16

If you had asked Paul, if Christ so actually lived in him that he no longer lived, what became of his responsibility? The answer was ready and clear: "I live by the faith of the Son of God, who loved me and gave Himself for me." His life was every moment a life of faith in Him who had loved him and given Himself so completely that He had undertaken at all times to be the life of His willing disciple.

WHY COULD WE NOT?

"The disciples ... said, Why could not we cast it out? He saith ... Because of your little faith ... this kind goeth not out but by prayer and fasting."
Matt. 17:19-21

To have a strong faith in God needs a life in close touch with Him by persistent prayer. We cannot call up faith at our bidding; it needs close communion with God. It needs not only prayer but fasting too in the larger and deeper meaning of that word. It needs the denial of self, the sacrifice of that pleasing of the flesh and the eye and the pride of life which is the essence of a worldly spirit.

THE POWER OF OBEDIENCE

*"He that hath sent Me is with Me;
He hath not left Me alone; for I do
always the things that are pleasing
to Him."*
John 8:29

Obedience is the proof and the exercise of
the love of God that has been shed abroad in
our hearts by the Holy Spirit. It comes from
love and leads to love, a deeper and a fuller
experience of God's love and indwelling. Christ
did not speak of an impossibility; He saw what
in the power of the Spirit we might confidently
expect.

THE POWER OF INTERCESSION

"We will continue steadfastly in prayer."
Acts 6:4

Immeasurably more important than any other work is the linking of all we do to the fountain of Divine life and energy. The Christian world has not only a right to expect mission leaders to set forth the facts and methods of the work, but also a larger discovery of superhuman resources and a greater irradiation of spiritual power. Shall we not, like the early Apostles, "continue steadfastly in prayer," until God sends an abundant answer?

THE POWER OF TIME

"My times are in Thy hand."
Ps. 31:15

The very essence of religion lies in the thought: Time with God. And yet how many of God's servants there are who frankly confess that the feebleness of their spiritual life as missionaries and the inadequate results of mission work as a whole are due to the failure to make the leisure and, when secured, rightly to use it for daily communion with God. Time spent alone with God will indeed bring into the lives of His servants the power to enable them to use all their time in His fellowship.

The Power of Faith

"All things are possible to him that believeth."
Mark 9:23

Think for a moment of what the marks of a true faith are. First of all, faith counts upon God to do all He has promised, as the only measure of its expectation. This is followed by a faith that begins to see that waiting on God is needed and that quietly rests in the hope of what God will do.

JOHN'S MISSIONARY MESSAGE

"That which we have seen and heard declare we unto you, that ye also may have fellowship with us: and truly our fellowship is with the Father, and with His Son Jesus Christ."
1 John 1:3

The message suggests that the very first duty of the minister or missionary every day is to maintain such close communion with God that he can preach the truth in the fullness of joy and with the consciousness that his life and conversation are the proof that his preaching is true, so that his words appeal with power.

PAUL'S MISSIONARY MESSAGE

"The mystery now made manifest to His saints: to whom God would make known what is the riches of the glory of this mystery among the Gentiles; which is Christ in you, the hope of glory."
Col. 1:26-27

To Paul's mind, the very centre and substance of his Gospel was the indwelling Christ. He spoke of the "riches of the glory of this mystery – Christ in you, the hope of glory." Though he had been so many years a preacher of this Gospel, he still asked for prayer, that he might make known that mystery aright.

THE MISSIONARY'S LIFE

*"Ye are witnesses, and God also,
how holily and righteously and
unblameably we behaved ourselves
toward you that believe."*
1 Thess. 2:10 R.V.

Let us believe that when Paul said, "Christ liveth in me," "I live no more," he spoke of an actual, divine, unceasing, abiding of Christ in him, working in him from hour to hour all that was well-pleasing to the Father. And let us not rest until we can say, "The Christ of Paul is my Christ! His missionary enduement is mine too."

THE HOLY SPIRIT

"The Comforter shall glorify Me: for He shall receive of Mine, and shall show it unto you."
John 16:14

Christ came as God to make known the Father, and the Spirit came as God to make known the Son in us. It is the Spirit who can deliver us from all the power of the flesh, who can conquer the power of the world. It is the Spirit through whom Christ Jesus will manifest Himself to us in nothing less than His abiding presence: "Lo, I am with you alway."

FILLED WITH THE SPIRIT

*"Be filled with the Spirit; speaking
one to another in psalms and
hymns and spiritual songs, singing
and making melody with your heart
to the Lord; giving thanks always for
all things."*
Eph. 5:18-20 R.V.

If we had the expression, "filled with the Spirit", only in regard to the story of Pentecost, we might naturally think that it was something special and not meant for ordinary life. But our text teaches us the great lesson that it is meant for every Christian and for everyday life.

The Christ Life

"Christ liveth in me."
Gal. 2:20
"Christ is our life."
Col. 3:4

Christ's life was more than His teaching, more than His work, more even than His death. It was His life in the sight of God and man that gave value to what He said and did and suffered. And it is this life, glorified in the resurrection, that He imparts to His people and enables them to live out before others. Everything depends upon the life with God in Christ being right.

AUGUST

The Christlike Life

"Have this mind in you, which was also in Christ Jesus."
Phil 2:5

And what was the mind that was in Christ Jesus? "Being in the form of God, He emptied Himself, taking the form of a servant, being made in the likeness of men; He humbled Himself, becoming obedient even unto death, yea, the death of the Cross." Self-emptying and self-sacrifice, obedience to God's will, and love to the world, such was the character of Christ for which God so highly exalted Him.

CHRIST: THE NEARNESS OF GOD

*"Draw nigh to God, and He will
draw nigh to you."*
James 4:8

That means, first of all, at the beginning of each day afresh to yield ourselves for His holy presence to rest upon us. It means giving time and all our heart and strength to allow Him to reveal Himself. It is impossible to expect the abiding presence of Christ with us through the day, unless there is the definite daily exercise of strong desire and childlike trust in His word: "Draw nigh to God, and He will draw nigh to you."

LOVE

*"Jesus, having loved His own
which were in the world, loved
them unto the end."*
John 13:1

Can words make it plainer that God's love to Christ is given to pass into us and to become our life, that the love wherewith the Father loved the Son is to be in us? If the Lord Jesus is to manifest Himself to us, it can only be to the loving heart. It is only in the atmosphere of a holy, living love that the abiding presence of the loving Christ can be known.

THE TRIAL AND TRIUMPH OF FAITH

"Jesus said unto him, If thou canst believe, all things are possible to him that believeth. And straightway the father of the child cried out, and said with tears, Lord, I believe; help Thou mine unbelief."
Mark 9:23-24

What a lesson! Of all things that are possible to faith, the most impossible is that I should be able to exercise such faith. The abiding presence of Christ is possible to faith. And this faith is possible to the soul that clings to Christ and trusts Him.

Exceeding Abundantly

"Now unto Him that is able to do exceeding abundantly above all that we ask or think, according to the power that worketh in us, unto Him be glory ..."
Eph. 3:20-21

Paul began his great prayer, "I bow my knees to the Father." He ends it by bringing us to our knees, to give glory to Him as able to fulfill every promise, to reveal Christ dwelling in our hearts and keep us in that life of love which leads to being filled with all the fullness of God. Child of God, bow in deep adoration, giving glory to God.

THE ONE THING NEEDFUL

"If it be asked, What this one thing is: *It is the Spirit of God brought again to His first power of life in us.*" Let us remember that it is of little profit to know the meaning of what we read; the great question is, whether we have taken the instruction to heart. Do we indeed believe that this is the one thing needful for the Church and ourselves so that the only thing that gives value to our religion is that it is the immediate work of the Spirit of God.

OUR TOTAL DEPENDENCE ON GOD ALONE

"The one relation, which is the ground alone of all true religion, is this; it is *a total unalterable dependence on God, an immediate continual receiving of every degree of goodness and happiness from God alone.* Nothing can be the good of religion, but the power and presence of God *really and essentially living and working in it.* So that the creature must have all its religious goodness as wholly and solely from God's immediate operation, as it had its first goodness at its creation."*

* William Law, *A Serious Call.*

Continual Inspiration

"No man can reach God with his love or have union with Him by it, *but he who is inspired with that one same Spirit of Love* with which God Himself loved from all eternity. Infinite hosts of new-created heavenly beings can begin no new kind of love to God, nor have the least power of beginning to love Him at all, but so far as *His own Holy Spirit of Love* is brought to life. *Therefore the continual inspiration or operation of the Holy Spirit is the one only possible ground of our continually loving God*."*

* William Law, *A serious Call*

The Spirit of God in Adam

"Now the thing itself, is *that first life of God which was essentially born in the soul of the first man, Adam* and to which he died. Therefore *immediate inspiration* is as necessary to make fallen man alive again unto God as it was to make man at first a living soul after the image of God. And *continual inspiration* is as necessary as man's continuance in his redeemed state. That alone which begins or gives life must of all necessity be the only continuance or preservation of life."*

* William Law, *A Serious Call.*

THE MINISTRATION OF THE SPIRIT

"Christ taught His disciples to expect the coming of a higher and more blessed state, which they could not have till *His outward teaching in human language was changed into the inspiration and operation of His Spirit in their souls.* As the Apostles could not, so no man can have any true and real knowledge of the spiritual blessings of Christ's redemption or fitness to preach and bear witness of them to the world, *but solely by that same Divine Spirit...*"*

* William Law, *A Serious Call.*

OUR DEATH AND LIFE IN CHRIST

"As the work of the Spirit consists in altering that which is the most radical in the soul, bringing forth a new spiritual death and a new spiritual life, it must be true that no one can know or believe the mysteries of Christ's redeeming power, but only and solely *by an inward and experimental finding and feeling the operation of them in that new death and new life, both* of which must be effected in the soul of man, or Christ is not known as its salvation."*

* William Law, *A Serious Call*.

HUMILITY

"In the whole nature of things nothing could be salvation or Savior to us, but such *a humility of God* manifested in human nature as is beyond all expression. Hence, the first unalterable Term of this Savior to fallen man is this, 'Except a man deny himself, forsakes all that he has, yea, and his own life, het cannot be My disciple.' Self is the whole evil of fallen nature; self-denial is our capacity of being saved, humility is our Savior."* *In the life of faith, humility has a far deeper place than we think. It is not only one among other virtues, but is the first and chief need of the soul.*

* William Law, *A Serious Call.*

THE KINGDOM OF HEAVEN

"'Thy Kingdom come, Thy will be done on earth as it is in heaven.' What is God's Kingdom in heaven but the *manifestation of what God is* and what He does in His heavenly creatures?"* *How much has been written about what the Kingdom of heaven means, but here we have what it really is. As God rules in His Kingdom in heaven, so when the kingdom comes into our hearts He lives and rules there. The Kingdom of God consists of those in whom God rules as He does in heaven.*

* William Law. *A Serious Call.*

The Nature of Love

"The Spirit of Love, wherever it is, is its own blessing and happiness, because it is the truth and the reality of God in the soul. For as love has no by-ends, wills nothing but its own increase, so everything is as oil to its flame. The Spirit of Love does not want to be rewarded or honored; its only desire is to propagate itself and become the blessing and happiness of everything that wants it."*

* William Law, *A Serious Call*.

THE NECESSITY OF LOVE

"The necessity therefore of the Spirit of Love is what God Himself cannot dispense with in the creature any more than He can deny Himself or act contrary to His own holy being. But as it was His Will to all Goodness that brought forth angels and the spirits of men, so He can will nothing in their existence but that they should live and work and manifest that same spirit of Love and Goodness which brought them into being."* *Let us take time to ponder this blessed truth and promise: the God and Father of all love is longing to fill the heart of His children with nothing less than His own Divine, Eternal Love!*

* William Law, *A Serious Call*.

LOVE: A NEW BIRTH FROM ABOVE

"Hold it therefore for a certain truth that you can have no good come into your soul, but only by the one way of a birth from above, from the *Entrance of the Deity* into the properties of your own soulish life. For Love is the one only blessing and goodness and God of nature; and you have no true religion or no worship of the one true God but in and by that Spirit of Love which is *God Himself living and working in you.*"*

* William Law, *A Serious Call.*

THE TWOFOLD LIFE

"No intelligent creature, whether angel or man, can be good and happy, but by partaking of and having in himself a twofold life. The twofold life is this: it must have the life of nature and the life of God in it. God Himself cannot make a creature to be in its self or as to its own nature anything else but a state of emptiness, of want, of appetite. The reason is this: it is because *goodness and happiness are absolutely inseparable from God* and can be nowhere but in God."*

* William Law, *A Serious Call.*

PERPETUAL INSPIRATION

"Perpetual inspiration therefore is in the nature of the thing as necessary to a life of Goodness, Holiness, and Happiness, as the perpetual respiration of the air is necessary to animal life. What a mistake it is to confine inspiration to particular times and occasions, to prophets and apostles when the common Christian looks and trusts *to be continually led and inspired by the Spirit of God*. If our thoughts and affections are to be always holy and good, then the Holy and Good Spirit of God is to be always operating as a principle of life within us."*

* William Law, *A Serious Call*.

TWO KINDS OF KNOWLEDGE

"Every kind of virtue and goodness may be brought into us by two different ways. They may be taught us outwardly by men, by rules and precepts; and they may be inwardly born in us as the genuine birth of our own renewed spirit. The Spirit of Prayer, the Spirit of Love, the Spirit of Humility are only to be obtained by the operation of *the Light and Spirit of God*, not outwardly teaching but *inwardly bringing forth a new-born spirit within us*." *

* William Law, *A Serious Call.*

THE MONSTER OF SELF

"If you ask what is this one true simple, plain, immediate, and unerring way, *it is the way of Patience, Meekness, Humility, and Resignation to God*. This is the truth and perfection of dying to self."* There is not a more difficult lesson in the Christian life than to attain a true knowledge of what self is. Its terrible power, its secret and universal rule, and the blinding influence it exerts in keeping us from the knowledge of what it is are the cause of all our sin and evil. Hence it comes that so few really believe in their absolute inability to obey God or to believe in His love.

* William Law, *A Serious Call.*

DYING TO SELF

"'Come unto Me, all ye that labor and are heavy laden, and I will give you rest.' How short and simple and certain a way to peace and comfort. When I exhort you to give up yourself in faith and hope to these virtues, what else do I do but turn you directly to so much faith and hope in the true Lamb of God."* *We too often think of faith in Christ only as connected with the work He did for us on the Cross. But its meaning is far larger and richer. It is by faith that we can claim all the grace and the mind there were in Him and receive it through the Spirit as ours.*

* William Law, *A Serious Call*.

AUGUST 22

Of Faith in Christ

"In the words of Christ, 'Learn of Me, for I am meek and lowly of heart, and ye shall find rest unto your souls,' you have two truths asserted. First that to be given up to Patience, Meekness, Humility, and Resignation to God is strictly the same thing as to learn of Christ or to have faith in Him. And that because the inclination of your heart toward these virtues is truly giving up all that you are and all that you have from fallen Adam, it is perfectly leaving all that you have and your highest act of faith in Him."*

* William Law, *A Serious Call.*

THE LAMB OF GOD

"This marriage-feast signifies the entrance into the highest state of union that can be between God and the soul in this life. In other words, it is the birthday of the Spirit of Love in our souls which, whenever we attain it, will feast our souls with such peace and joy in God as will blot out the remembrance of everything that we called joy or peace before. As the Lamb of God He has all power to bring forth in us a weariness of our fallen state and a willingness to fall from it into His Meekness and Humility."*

* William Law, *A Serious Call.*

PRAYER: THE KEY TO THE TREASURES OF HEAVEN

"Man has been sent into the world on no other errand but by prayer to rise out of the vanity of time into the riches of eternity. For poor and miserable as this life is, we have all of us free access to all that is great and good and happy and carry within ourselves *a key to all the treasures that Heaven has to bestow upon us*." *

* William Law, *A Serious Call*.

THE GOODNESS OF GOD

"This is the amiable nature of God; He is the Good, the unchangeable overflowing fountain of good, that sends forth nothing but good to all eternity."* *With what joy an invalid on a winter's day yields himself to bask in the bright sunshine. What journeys are undertaken to the heights in Switzerland where the sun gives its warmth best. And, alas! how little God's children understand that this is just the one thing they need, to wait before God in quiet till His light shines upon them and into them and through them.*

* William Law, *A Serious Call.*

THE KINGDOM OF SELF

"Man by his fall had fallen from a life in God *into a life of self,* an animal life of self-love, self-esteem, and self-seeking in the poor perishing enjoyments of the world. All sin, death, and hell are nothing else but this kingdom of self or the various operations of self-love, self-esteem, and self-seeking."* *Let us take hold of the central thought here that to make way for the immediate and continual operation of God in our souls, we need in the power of the Holy Spirit absolutely to renounce self and yield our whole being for God to dwell and work in.*

* William Law, *A Serious Call.*

CONTINUAL SELF—DENIAL

"To think of anything in religion or to pretend to real holiness *without totally dying to this old man* is building castles in the air. To think of being alive in God before we are dead to our own nature is as impossible as for a grain of wheat to be alive before it dies."* Our blessed Lord Jesus could not be raised from the dead into the glory of the Father's right hand until He had died on the Cross. This is the new and living way which He opened up through the rent veil of the flesh into the Holiest of All.

* William Law, *A Serious Call.*

PRAYER: A STATE OF THE HEART

It would be worthwhile making a study of the place that, according to Law, the word "continual" ought to have in our life. First there is the continual streaming forth of the infinite love of God toward us. Then the continual unalterable dependence upon God every hour of our life. Then the continual receiving of goodness and happiness from God alone. Then the continual mortification of our evil nature; then the continual and immediate inspiration of the Holy Spirit maintaining the Life of Christ in us. Then the continual breathing of the heart after God in prayer, and then the continual loving of Him with our whole heart.

A WORLDLY SPIRIT

"For a worldly, earthly spirit can know nothing of God. All real knowledge is Life or a living sensibility of the thing that is known as far as our life reaches, so far we understand and know, and no further. All after this is only the play of our imagination amusing itself with the dead pictures of its own ideas."* *When our Lord spoke of the world, its prince, and its spirit, He ever laid stress on its hatred of Him and His Church. And so His Apostles, too, warned most earnestly against being conformed to the world.* "If a man love the world, the love of the Father is not in him."

* William Law, *A Serious Call.*

OF THE DESPAIR OF SELF

"But till all is despair in ourselves, faith and hope and turning to God in prayer are only things practiced by rule and method; they are not born in us, are not living qualities of a new birth till we have done feeling any trust or confidence in ourselves."* *Let us seek above everything to believe that God is love and as such longs intensely to fill every heart with its blessedness. As the sun shines upon the earth with the one great object of shedding on it its light and its life, do let us believe that the great God of love is shining upon us every moment of the day.*

* William Law, *A Serious Call.*

True Religion

"Here you should once for all mark where and what the true nature of religion is; its work and effect is *within*, its glory, its life, its perfection is all within. It is merely and solely the raising a new life, new love, and a new birth in the inward spirit of our heart. It is nothing else *but the power and life and Spirit of God*, as Father, Son, and Holy Spirit working, creating, and reviving life in the fallen soul and driving all its evil out of it." * Oh, let us seek to study what God counts true religion. Nothing less than this, that He Himself, by His Spirit, should live and work in us as the Light and the Life of our souls.

* William Law, *A Serious Call.*

SEPTEMBER

THE PRACTICE OF PRAYER

What a universal confession there is that we pray too little. How strange that our highest privilege, holding fellowship with God in prayer, is to so many a burden and a failure and to so many more a matter of form without the power. Let us learn the lesson that to expect nothing from ourselves is the first step and then truly with the heart to expect everything from God. These two thoughts lie at the root of all true prayer.

A Touchstone of Truth

"I will here give you an infallible touchstone that will tie all to the truth. It is this: retire from the world and all conversation. Offer this one prayer to God: 'That of His great goodness, He would make known to you and take from your heart every kind and form and degree of pride, whether it be from evil spirits or your own corrupt nature and that He would awaken in you the deepest depths and truth of that humility which can make you capable of His light and His Holy Spirit.'"[1]*

* William Law, *A Serious Call.*

The Spirit of Prayer

"The spirit of the soul is in itself nothing else but a spirit breathed forth from the life of God and for this only end, that the life of God, the nature of God, the working of God the tempers of God might be manifested in it. The Spirit of Prayer is a pressing forth of the soul out of this earthly life; it is a stretching with all its desires after the life of God; it is a leaving, as far as it can, all its own spirit to receive a Spirit from above, to be one Life, one Love, one Spirit with Christ in God."*

* William Law, *A Serious Call.*

THE PRAYER OF THE HEART

"Turning to God according to the inward feeling, want, and motion of your own heart in love, in trust, in faith of having from Him all that you want and wish to have – this turning unto God, whether it be with or without words, is the best form of prayer in the world. For prayers not formed according to the real state of your heart are but like a prayer to be pulled out of a deep well when you are not in it."*

* William Law, *A Serious Call*.

THE PROOF OF THE SPIRIT

"The Holy Spirit of God is as necessary to our Divine life as the air of this world is necessary to our animal life and is as distinct from and as much without us as the air of this world is distinct from the creatures that live in it. And yet our own good spirit is the very Spirit of God moving and stirring in us, and yet not God, but the Spirit of God breathed into a creaturely form; and this good Spirit, Divine in its origin, and Divine in its nature, is that alone in us that can reach God, unite with Him, be moved and blessed by Him. 'Hereby we know that He abideth in us, by the Spirit which He hath given us.'" *

* William Law. *A Serious Call.*

LOVE AND FAITH

"This is His commandment, that we should believe in the name of His Son Jesus Christ, and love one another, even as He gave us commandment."
1 John 3:23

The Church must learn not only to preach the love of God in redemption; it must go further and teach Christians to show that the love of Christ is in their hearts by love shown to the brethren. Our Lord called this a new commandment – a badge by which the world should recognize His disciples!

FAITH AND LOVE

*"And the grace of our Lord
abounded exceedingly with
faith and love."*
1 Tim. 1:14

*"Your faith groweth exceedingly,
and the love of each of you all
toward one another aboundeth."*
2 Thess. 1:3

These expressions of the Apostle Paul show us the true connection between faith and love in the life of the Christian. Faith always comes first; it roots itself deeply in the love of God and bears fruit in love to the brethren. As in nature the root and the fruit are inseparable, so is it with faith and love in the realm of grace.

THE LOVE OF GOD

"God is love, and he that dwelleth in love dwelleth in God, and God in him."
1 John 4:16

The God who wills nothing but good is a God of love. He does not seek His own; He does not live for Himself but pours out His love on all living creatures. The characteristic of Love is that she "seeketh not her own." She finds her happiness in giving to others; she sacrifices herself wholly for others. *This self-same love of God, Christ has poured into our hearts through the Holy Spirit* so that our whole life may be permeated with its vital power.

THE LOVE OF CHRIST

*"The love of Christ
constraineth us."*
2 Cor. 5:14

God's desire is that on this sinful earth, likewise, His love should take possession of our hearts. O Christians, think this over: God longs to have our hearts wholly filled with His love. Then He will be able to use us as channels for this love to flow out to others. Let us say with the Apostle Paul: "The love of Christ constraineth me" (Dutch Version – "urges").

THE LOVE OF THE SPIRIT

*"The love of God hath been
shed abroad in our hearts
through the Holy Spirit,
which was given unto us."*
Rom. 5:5

Learn the lesson of our text: "The love of God hath been shed abroad in our hearts, through the Holy Spirit." The Spirit will enable us to love God and other Christians and even our enemies. Be assured of two things. First, that in your own strength you cannot love God or other Christians. And, second, that the Holy Spirit is within you every day and every hour, to fill you with the Spirit of love.

THE POWER OF LOVE

*"We are more that conquerors
through Him that loved us."*
Rom. 8:37

In days of unrest and strong racial feeling, we need above all a new discovery and living experience of the love of God. Let us anchor our hope in the thought, "God is Love." God's power by which He rules and guides the world is the power of an undying, persistent love. He works through the hearts and spirits and wills of men and women wholly yielded to Him and His service; and He waits for them to open their hearts to Him in love and then, full of courage, to become witnesses for Him.

THE SIGN OF A TRUE CHURCH

"By this shall all men know that ye are My disciples, if ye have love one to another."
John 13:35

In God, love reaches its highest point and is the culmination of His glory. In the man Christ Jesus on the cross, love is at its highest. We owe everything to this love. Love is the power that moved Christ to die for us. In love, God highly exalted Him as Lord and Christ. Love is the power that broke our hearts, and love is the power that heals them. Love is the power through which Christ dwells in us and works in us.

RACE—HATRED

*"For we also were sometimes
foolish, living in malice and envy,
hateful, and hating one another."*
Titus 3:3

No wonder that man's love of his own people,
implanted in his heart by nature, soon changed
to hatred of other peoples. Love of country
became the fruitful source of race-hatred, war,
and bloodshed. What an opening there is for the
Church of Christ and her ministers to preach
and proclaim the love of God and to prove its
might to change race-hatred into brotherly
love! God has abundant power to bring this to
pass.

"LOVE YOUR ENEMIES"

*"Thou shalt love thy neighbor
and hate thine enemy."*
Matt. 5:43

It was the Jewish Rabbis in Christ's earthly day who said this. How often the Christian follows the example of the Jewish teachers! The command of our Lord is too strict and narrow for us; we have not yielded ourselves to God in obedience to the new commandment to love other Christians with Christ's love, believing that this love will flow out to all around, even to those who hate us. This will require much grace and will cost time and trouble and much earnest prayer.

Forgive, but Not Forget

"I will forgive their iniquity, and I will remember their sin no more."
Jer. 31:34

"Forgive – yes, but forget – never." Many have allowed themselves to be deceived by these words. I have often seen a dog come in at the front door to seek coolness. He would be driven out, and the door closed but would go in again through the back door. The front door is: "I will forgive." But see how quickly and quietly these evil thoughts come back through the back door of "I will never forget." Many a one trusts in God's forgiving love, but does not remember that when God forgives, He forgets.

As God Forgives

*"And forgive us our sins; for we
also forgive every one that is
indebted to us."*
Luke 11:4

The forgiveness of sins is the great all-embracing gift by which, in His mercy, God sets the sinner free and receives him back into His love and favor. It gives us boldness toward God and is the source of our salvation; it gives us cause for thankfulness every day. It is God's will and our souls feel the need of it, that we should each day walk with Him, as those whose sins are forgiven and who are living in the light of His countenance.

The Preaching of Love

"The greatest of these is Love."
1 Cor. 13:13

Often in preaching or in writing, I have asked myself: But do you possess what you preach to others? And I have followed the advice: *Preach it because you believe it to be the teaching of God's Word, and heartily desire it.* Preach the truth by faith, and the experience will follow. Let the minister who feels impelled to preach about love not hesitate to do so, and he will soon be able to preach it because he has himself received that which he commends.

THE LEADERS

"I exhort, therefore, that first of all supplications, prayers, intercessions, thanksgivings, be made for all men; for kings and all that are in authority, ..."
1 Tim. 2:1-2

We must pray for our leaders and for *all* who are in authority. As leaders of the people, their influence for good or evil is inexpressible. Their hearts are in God's hands, and He can turn them whithersoever He wills. Let our prayers ascend to God in all sincerity, and He will hear and grant that which is good for the whole land.

UNFEIGNED LOVE
OF THE BRETHREN

"Seeing ye have purified your souls through the Spirit, unto unfeigned love of the brethren, see that ye love one another with a pure heart ..."
1 Peter 1:22

God's Word is a mirror into which the Church and each individual member must look, to see that we are truly Christian, showing by our conduct that we take God's Word as our rule of life. If our hearts condemn us, we must turn at once to God, confessing our sin. Let us believe that *the Spirit of love does indeed dwell in us.*

THE SPIRIT OF LOVE

"The fruit of the Spirit is love."
Gal. 5:22
"God hath given us the spirit of love."
2 Tim. 1:7

This divine love in the heart of the believer is *a little sanctuary, whence the child of God receives power,* in obedience to the inner law of love, to live always in the love of God. This holy love includes Fellowship with God, Union with Christ, and Love to all Christians. How can we attain to this experience? Through *faith alone.*

A Song of Love

*"But now abideth faith, hope, love,
these three; but the greatest of
these is love."*
1 Cor. 13:13

Love is the greatest thing in the world. We should read this chapter oftener than we do and commit the Song to memory so that the great words are imprinted on our hearts: "Love seeketh not her own." Think over it and pray over it. "Love never faileth." Consider all that means. "The greatest of these is love." Let this love rule in your life. Thus you will be a fountain of blessing to all around you.

THE OBEDIENCE OF LOVE

"If ye love Me, ye will keep My commandments."
John 14:15

This precept loses its power because Christians say: "It is quite impossible; I cannot always keep His commandments." And so conscience is quieted, and the commandments are not kept. Yet our Lord really meant it, for in the last night with His disciples, He promised them definitely a new life in which the power of the Spirit would enable them to live a life of obedience.

LOVE AND PRAYER

*"Be sober, and watch unto prayer,
above all things being fervent in
your love among yourselves."*
1 Peter 4:7-8

In our text, watching unto prayer and fervent love are closely linked. This is true, too, in the spiritual life. The man who prays only for himself will not find it easy to be in the right attitude toward God. But where the heart is filled with fervent love to others, prayer will continually rise to God for those whom we love and even for those with whom we do not agree.

The First and Great Commandment

"... to love the Lord the God with all thy heart and with all thy soul."
Deut. 30:6

God greatly desires our love. But how can I attain such a condition – *through faith alone.* When we take time to wait upon God and remember with what a burning desire God sought to win our love through the gift of His Son, we shall be able to realize that God has a strong and never-ceasing longing for the love of our heart.

THE ROYAL LAW OF LOVE

"If ye fulfill the royal law according to the scripture, Thou shalt love thy neighbor as thyself, ye do well."
James 2:8

When our Lord, in answer to the question, "Master, which is the great commandment in the law?" had answered: "Thou shalt love the Lord thy God with all thy heart," He added: "The second is like unto it, Thou shalt love thy neighbor as thyself." These two commandments both contain the one verb, love. In heaven where God is and on earth among all people, love is the royal law, love is supreme.

NATIONAL FEELING

"God hath made of one blood all nations of men."
Acts 17:26

"Every creature of God is good, for it is sanctified by the Word and by prayer." Without that sanctifying process, national feeling may become the prey of ambition and the source of hatred, aversion and comtempt for other nations. It is the holy calling of every Christian, and minister of the Gospel, to point out the way by which national feeling may attain its twofold aim: (1) the development and uplifting of the people themselves, and (2) the right attitude to other peoples in the upbuilding of all mankind.

ONE STREAM OR TWO STREAMS?

"The stick of Ephraim, and the stick of Judah, I will make them ons stick, and they shall be one in Mine hand."
Ezek. 37:19

When Ephraim and Judah bacame one in God's hand, the difference between the two was not destroyed. Each kept separate characteristics but also the oneness was that of true unity and mutual love. God will fulfill this promise to us but on one condition: We must place our people in God's hand by our prayers.

PRAY FOR LOVE

*"The Lord make you to increase
and abound in love one toward
another, and toward all men, ..."*
1 Thess. 3:12

As the sun freely gives its light and heat to the grass and grain that they may grow and bring forth fruit, so God is far more willing to give His love to us in ever-increasing measure. O Christian, if you feel as if you cannot pray, take these words of divine love and ponder them in your heart. You will gain a strong and a joyous assurance of what God is able to do for you. He will make you to abound in love and strengthen yout heart to live before Him in holiness.

LIKE CHRIST

"I have given you an example, that ye should do as I have done to you."
John 13:15

Faith in Christ's wonderful love and in God's inconceivable love resting upon us, makes it not only possible but certain that those who keep close to Christ will walk in love. What a blessed life in the love and the power that we have in Christ! What a blessed walk in His fellowship, when we are led by the Holy Spirit and strengthened for a life in His likeness!

THE POWER OF GOD'S WORD

"The words that I have spoken unto you are spirit and are life."
John 6:63

It is necessary to be deeply convinced of our utter inability to produce this love which is holy and can conquer sin and unbelief. We need *a burning desire to receive this heavenly love into our hearts* whatever the cost may be. Then at length we shall gain an insight into what God's Word is as a living power in our hearts. This supernatural power will be the love of God shed abroad in our hearts by the Holy Spirit living and working within us.

OCTOBER

PERFECT LOVE ACCORDING TO 1 JOHN

*"He that loveth his brother
abideth in the light."*
1 John 2:10

Each of these words is a living seed and has within it a Divine power which is able to take root and grow and bear fruit in our hearts. But just as the seed requires the soil in which it grows to be kept free of all weeds, so the heart must be wholly surrendered to God and His service, that the seed of the Word may bear this heavenly fruit.

THE LOVE THAT SUFFERS

*"Walk in love, as Christ also
hath loved us, and hath
given Himself for us."*
Eph. 5:2

Is it not strange that love, which is the source of the greatest happiness, should also be the cause of intense suffering? Our life on earth is such that suffering always follows when love seeks to save the object of its love. It is only by means of suffering that love can gain its end and so attain the highest happiness. What a wonderful thought! Even the almighty power of God's love could not achieve its purpose without suffering that passes understanding.

THE WORKS OF THE FLESH

"The works of the flesh are manifest; witchcraft, hatred, strife, jealousies, wrath, envyings, murders, and such like."
Gal. 5:19-21

Learn these three great lessons: 1. Christians cannot in their own strength love God and all people. 2. The great reason of so much bitterness and want of love, is that Christians walk after the flesh. 3. The only sure way to love God and Christ with the whole heart, to love one another fervently, and to have a tender compassionate love for all who do not yet know Christ – is an absolute surrender to the Holy Spirit.

PASSING THE LOVE OF WOMEN

"My brother Jonathan: ...
thy love to me was wonderful,
passing the love of women."
2 Sam. 1:26

God created man in order to show what the power of love is when a man strives for the welfare of others and even gives up his life for them. He created woman to show what tenderness and quiet endurance are when she sacrifices herself for the sake of others. But one must not forget that the best ornament of a woman is a meek and quiet spirit which is of great price in the sight of God and of man and which makes her a blessing in her home.

STEWARDS OF THE LOVE OF GOD

"Moreover it is required in stewards, that a man be found faithful."
1 Cor. 4:2

A steward is the man to whom the king or master entrusts his treasures and goods. The minister of the Gospel is a steward of God and above all of the deep mystery of His everlasting love and all the blessings that flow from it. So the minister of the Gospel must himself be faithful not only to God, but to his congregation.

FAITH WORKING THROUGH LOVE

*"In Christ Jesus neither circumcision
availeth anything, nor
uncircumcision; but faith
working through love."*
Gal. 5:6

Faith is the root; Love is the fruit. Faith becomes strong in the love of God and of Christ. Faith in God and love to the brethren must always go hand in hand. O Christian, the whole of salvation lies in these two words – Faith and Love. Let our faith each day take deeper root in God's eternal love. And then each day the fruit of the Spirit will be love in all our dealings with those around us.

THE DISPENSATION OF THE SPIRIT

"How much more shall your Heavenly Father give the Holy Spirit to them that ask Him."
Luke 11:13

The main thing for us is to receive, afresh from the Father, the Holy Spirit for our daily needs and daily life. Without this we cannot please God, nor can we be of any real help to those around us. Water cannot rise higher than its source. And so it happens that if the Holy Spirit prays through us, as human channels, our prayers will rise again to God who is their source, and the prayers will be answered by the Divine working in ourselves and in others.

The Fruit Of The Spirit

*"The fruit of the Spirit is love,
joy, peace, long-suffering,
gentleness, goodness, faith,
meekness, temperance."*
Gal. 5:22-23

Think of the first three fruits, *Love, Joy, Peace*, the three chief characteristics of a strong faith life. *Love* to God and to Christ, to other Christians and to all people. *Joy*, the proof of the perfect fulfillment of every need, of courage and faith for all the work we have to do. *Peace*, the blessed state of undisturbed rest and security in which the peace of God that passes all understanding can keep our hearts and minds.

LED BY THE SPIRIT

"As many as are led by the Spirit of God, they are the sons of God."
Rom. 8:14

Let us now consider four other fruits of the Spirit: *Long-suffering, Gentleness, Goodness, Meekness,* all denoting attributes of the Godhead. They will reach maturity in us through much prayer for the working of the Holy Spirit. Is it not a wonderful thought that these four attributes of God, which are the characteristics of God's work among sinners, may be brought to ripeness in our hearts by the Holy Spirit, so that we in all our ways and conversation may be like the Meek and Lowly One.

THE SPIRIT OF FAITH

*"Having the same spirit of
faith, we also believe."*
2 Cor. 4:13

Let us pause a while on the two last fruits of the Spirit – *Faith and Temperance*. *Faith* is a fruit of the Spirit – and leads the seeking soul to depend on God alone. Faith believes God's Word and clings to Him and waits in perfect trust that His Power will work within us all that He has promised. *Temperance* refers in the first place to eating and drinking and leads us to restraint, carefulness, and unselfishness in our conversation, our desires, in all our dealings with one another.

WORSHIP GOD IN SPIRIT

"We are the circumcision, which worship God in the Spirit, and rejoice in Christ Jesus, and have no confidence in the flesh."
Phil. 3:3

Our text says: "We serve God in the Spirit, we glory in the Lord Jesus, and have no confidence in the flesh." We have no power to do the thing that is good. We count on the Lord Jesus through the Holy Spirit to work within us. Let us take time to think and meditate on these things. It will help to strengthen our faith if we repeat the text of Galatians 5:22, asking God to grant these fruits in our lives.

Intercession

"Pray one for another."
James 5:16

Let us learn the lesson thoroughly: Prayer should not be for ourselves alone, but chiefly for others. Let us begin by praying for those who are near and dear to us, those with whom we live, that we may be of help to them and not a hindrance. Pray for divine wisdom, for thoughtfulness for others, for kindliness, for self-sacrifice on their behalf.

TIME

*"What, could ye not watch
with me one hour?."*
Matt. 26:40

Dear child of God, let us never say, "I have no time for God." Let the Holy Spirit teach us that the most important, the most blessed, the most profitable time of the whole day is the time we spend alone with God. Pray to the Lord Jesus who in His earthly life experienced the need of prayer, pray to the Holy Spirit who will impress upon us this divine truth. Whatever else is left undone, God has the first and chief right to my time.

THE WORD OF GOD

*"The Word of God is
living and active.."*
Heb. 4:12

Prayer is like fire. The fire can only burn brightly if it is supplied with good fuel. That fuel is God's Word which must not only be studied carefully and prayerfully, but must be taken into the heart and lived out in the life. The inspiration and powerful working of the Holy Spirit alone can do this.

In the Name of Christ

"Whatsoever ye do, in word or in deed, do all in the Name of the Lord Jesus, giving thanks to God the Father through Him."
Col. 3:17

I have often spoken and written of what it means to pray in the Name of Christ. On reading our text of today I thought: Here we have the right explanation. The man who does all in word and deed, in the Name of Jesus, may have the full, childlike confidence that what he asks in that Name, he will receive. Take the text into your heart, and you may count on the Holy Spirit to make it true in your life.

The Spirit Glorifies Christ

"He shall glorify Me, for He shall take of Mine, and shall declare it unto you."
John 16:14

Where there is an earnest desire for the glory of Jesus in the heart of the believer, the Holy Spirit will preserve the holy Presence of Jesus in our hearts all the day. We must not weary ourselves with striving after God's Presence. Then shall we be able to count upon the secret but powerful working of the Spirit within us.

PRAYING IN THE SPIRIT

*"Praying in the Spirit, keep your-
selves in the love of God."*
Jude 20-21

The Holy Spirit will not come to us, nor work within us, just at certain times when we think we need His aid. The Spirit comes to be our life-companion. He wants us wholly in His possession at all times, otherwise He cannot do His work in us. Many Christians do not grasp the truth that He must dwell in them continually and have full possession of all their being. When once this truth is grasped, we shall realize that it is possible to live always "praying in the Spirit."

The Temple of God

"Know ye not, that ye are the temple of God, and that the Spirit of God dwelleth in you? The temple of God is holy, which temple ye are."
1 Cor. 3:16-17

From eternity it was God's desire to create man for a dwelling in which to show forth His glory. It is through the Holy Spirit that you will be sanctified into a temple of God, and you will experience that Christ, with the Father, will take up His abode in your heart. Do you desire that the Holy Spirit should teach you to pray? He will do it on this one condition, that you surrender yourself wholly to His guidance.

THE FELLOWSHIP OF THE SPIRIT

*"The Communion of the
Holy Spirit be with you."*
2 Cor. 13:14

In this verse we have one of the chief characteristics and activities of the Holy Spirit. It is the Holy Spirit through whom the Father and Son are one and through whom they have fellowship with each other in the Godhead. For the Holy Spirit is the true life of the Godhead. Through the Spirit we know and experience the fellowship of love in the life with the Father and Son.

WITH THE WHOLE HEART

"Ye shall seek Me, and find Me, when ye shall search for Me with all your heart."
Jer. 29:13

If one seeks to perform any great work, he must do it *with his whole heart and with all his powers*. In worldly affairs this is the secret of success and victory. And above all in divine things, it is indispensable, especially in praying for the Holy Spirit. Have you ever realized when you pray for the Holy Spirit, *that you are praying for the whole Godhead to take possession of you?* Child of God, the Holy Spirit longs to possess you wholly.

THE LOVE OF GOD IN OUR HEARTS

"The love of God hath been shed abroad in our hearts through the Holy Spirit, which is given unto us."
Rom. 5:5

It takes time to believe in the divine mighty working of the Holy Spirit through whom our hearts are filled with the love of God. We need time for retirement from the world and its interests for our souls to bask in the light of God so that the eternal love may take possession of our hearts. If you long for this, draw nigh to God in quiet worship and adoration.

WALK IN THE SPIRIT

"Walk in the Spirit ... If we live in the Spirit, let us also walk in the Spirit."
Gal. 5:16, 25

People speak as though the Spirit were only needed in our communion with God when we pray or for our work in the service of the Kingdom. This is a great mistake. God gives us His Spirit to be in us the whole day. We need Him most in the midst of our daily work because the world has then such power to lead us away from God. We need to pray the Father every morning for a fresh portion of His Spirit for each day.

THE SPIRIT PROMISED TO THE OBEDIENT

"If ye love Me, ye will keep My commandments. And I will pray the Father, and He shall give you another Comforter."
John 14:15-16

The Lord tells us here on what conditions He will send the Spirit. The Holy Spirit is given us to enable us to do the will of the Father. The condition is reasonable and just, that as far as we have kept the commandments through the Spirit, the Spirit will be granted to us in fuller measure.

SPIRITUAL OR CARNAL?

*"And I, brethren, could not
speak unto you as unto spiritual,
but as unto carnal, even as
unto babes in Christ."*
1 Cor. 3:1

God calls us and the Spirit draws us to be spiritual men and women – that is to say, people who pray each day to be led and guided each day into a truly spiritual life. Do not serve God half-heartedly.

THE SPIRIT OF WISDOM

*"That the Father may give unto you
a spirit of wisdom and revelation in
the knowledge of Him, ..."*
Eph. 1:17-18

There is a divine side in which the holy God expresses His deepest thoughts to us. Only through the Holy Spirit can the Christian appropriate the divine truth contained in God's Word. Paul prays earnestly that God would grant the spirit of wisdom to his readers, eyes that are enlightened through the Holy Spirit to understand what is written and to know the exceeding greatness of His power working in all who believe.

THE SPIRIT OF SANCTIFICATION

"Elect, through sanctification of the Spirit, unto obedience and sprinkling of the blood of Christ."
1 Peter 1:2

But when you once understand that He has the name of Holy Spirit in order definitely to impart God's holiness and will sanctify you wholly, then you will begin to realize that the Holy Spirit dwells in your heart. And what will be the result? You will feel that He must have you wholly. He must rule and control the whole day. My whole life and conversation must be in the Spirit.

RIVERS OF LIVING WATER

*"He that believeth on Me, out of him
shall flow rivers of living water."*
John 7:38

What do we need in order to experience these two wonderful promises of the well of water and the rivers of living water? Just one thing – *the inner attachment to Christ and the unreserved surrender to fellowship with Him and the firm assurance that His Spirit will work in us what we cannot do.* In one word: He that believeth on Me. We need a faith that rejoices in the divine might and love and depends on Him day by day to grant us grace that living water may flow forth from us.

JOY IN GOD

"For the kingdom of God is righteouness and peace and joy in the Holy Spirit."
Rom. 14:17

Truly a significant lesson. Many Christians do not understand that the joy of the Lord will keep them and fit them for their work. To many the thought of the Holy Spirit is a matter of grief and self-reproach, of desire and disappointment, of something too high and holy for them. What a foolish thought, that the great gift of the Father, meant to keep us in the joy and peace of Christ, should be a matter of self-reproach and care!

All the Day — Every Day

"Every day will I bless Thee."
Ps. 145:2

A man who had undergone a serious operation asked his doctor, "How long will I have to lie here?" And the answer came: "Only a day at a time." And that is the law of the Christian life. God gave the manna daily, the morning and evening sacrifice on the altar — by these God showed that His children should live by the day. Seek this day to trust to the leading of the Holy Spirit the whole day. You need not care for the morrow, but rest in the assurance that He who has led you today will draw still nearer tomorrow.

THE SPIRIT AND THE CROSS

*"The blood of Christ, who
through the Eternal Spirit offered
Himself without blemish unto God,
shall cleanse your conscience ..."*
Heb. 9:14

How is it so few Christians understand or experience that the fellowship of the Spirit is a fellowship of the cross? Simply because they do not feel the need of praying for the Spirit of wisdom to give them a deep, spiritual insight into the oneness of the Spirit and the Cross. They try to use their human understanding, but there is too little waiting upon God to teach them divine truths through the Spirit.

The Spirit and the Blood

> *"There are three who bear witness, the Spirit, and the water, and the blood: and these three agree in one."*
> 1 John 5:8

The water is external, a sign of the renewing and purifying through regeneration used in baptism. The Spirit and the blood are two spiritual expressions, working together in regeneration: the blood for the forgiveness of sins, the Spirit for the renewal of the whole nature. All through life the Spirit and the blood must agree. The oneness is spiritual and true. Through the blood we obtain the Spirit.

NOVEMBER

The Spirit in Preacher and Hearer

"Our Gospel came unto you ... in power, and in the Holy Spirit ..."
1 Thess. 1:5

We, as hearers, are so accustomed to listen attentively to the sermon to see what it has to teach us, that we are apt to forget the prayer for the preacher that he may speak "in the demonstration of the Spirit", and then the prayer for ourselves, that we may receive the Word, not from man, but as it is in truth.

THE FULL GOSPEL

"Then Peter said: Repent, ... for the remission of sins, and ye shall receive the gift of the Holy Spirit."
Acts 2:38

How often only half the Gospel is preached – conversion and forgiveness of sins, and souls are led no further into the truth – the knowledge and appropriation of the life of the Spirit within us is not mentioned. No wonder that so many Christians fail to understand that they must depend each day on the Spirit for the joy which will be their strength.

THE MINISTRY OF THE SPIRIT

"Ye are an epistle of Christ, ministered by us, written with the Spirit of the living God, ..."
2 Cor. 3:3

Oh, that God would restore the ministry of the Gospel to its original power! Oh, that all ministers and church-members would unite in the prayer that God, by the mighty working of His Spirit, would give the ministry of the Spirit its right place and teach the people to believe that when Christ is preached to them, they are beholding as in a glass the glory of the Lord and may be changed into the same image by the Spirit of the Lord!

THE SPIRIT FROM HEAVEN

"Them that preached the gospel unto you by the Holy Spirit sent down from heaven."
1 Peter 1:12

Christ has taught us to think of God as our own Father in heaven who is ready to bestow His blessings on His children on earth. O Christian, take time each day to receive from the Father the continual guidance of the Holy Spirit. Do not be unbelieving. The Holy Spirit will do His part, if you in faith surrender yourself to His control.

THE SPIRIT AND PRAYER

*"Verily, Verily, I say unto you, If ye
shall ask anything of the Father, in
My Name, He will give it you."*
John 16:23

In our Lord's farewell discourse (John 13:17)
He presented the life in the dispensation of the
Spirit in all its power and attractiveness. One of
the most glorious results of the day when the
Holy Spirit should come would be: *the new
power that man should have* to pray down from
heaven the power of God to bless the world.
Seven times we have the promise repeated:
"Whatsoever ye shall desire in My Name, *that
will I do."*

With One Accord in Prayer

*"These all with one accord
continued steadfastly in prayer."*
Acts 1:14

O Christian, *daily prayer in fellowship with God's children is indispensable*, and it is a sacred duty if the Spirit is again to come in power. Let not your knowledge of the working of God's Holy Spirit be limited to yourself alone nor even to your Church, but in a world-embracing love of Christ for all God's children and His kingdom over the whole world, pray for power.

GOD'S PLAN OF SALVATION

*"When Christ, who is our life, shall
be manifested, then shall ye also
with Him be manifested in glory ."*
Col. 3:4

The full Gospel is contained in these words:
"Christ is our life." Many Christians forget this.
They believe Christ died on the cross for them
and lives in Heaven for them, but hardly that
Christ is in them. The powerlessness of the
Church is mainly due to this. *We do not realize
that the Almighty Christ dwells in us.* We must
know and experience and testify to this great
truth if there is to be a real and lasting revival
in the Church of Christ.

THE TWOFOLD LIFE

*"I Came that they may have life,
and may have it abundantly."*
John 10:10

Everyone can understand the difference between life that is weak and sickly and life that has abundant vitality. Thus St. Paul speaks of the Christian life of the Corinthians as not spiritual but carnal, as of young children in Christ incapable of assimilating strong meat or understanding the deeper truths of the Gospel. There are some, the majority of Christians, who never advance beyond first principles. Dear Reader, ask yourself if you are living such an abundant life as Jesus came to bestow?

LIFE ABUNDANT

*"Where sin abounded, grace
did abound more exceedingly:
that, as sin reigned in death,
even so might grace reign ..."*
Rom. 5:20-21

These words of the Holy Spirit are almost
beyond our grasp. Let us continually take them
to God that He Himself through His Holy Spirit
may make them to live in our hearts. With such
a God, with such abounding grace – much
more abundant than the easily besetting sin –
with such a Lord Jesus to give grace and cause
grace to reign – thank God, I may believe that
life abundant is for me!

"Christ Liveth in Me"

"I have been crucified with Christ; yet I live: and yet no longer I, but Christ liveth in me."
Gal. 2:20

In these words St. Paul expresses three great thoughts: Firstly, "I am crucified with Christ." Secondly, "I live, and yet no longer I." His third thought, "Christ liveth in me," is the true secret of a Christlike life. Christ was not only crucified for me. He does not live only in heaven to intercede for me. No! Christ *liveth in me*. He Himself said that even as His Father dwelt and worked in Him, even so He dwells and works in us.

THE LIFE OF FAITH

"That life which I now live in the flesh I live in faith, the faith which is in the Son of God, who loved me, and gave Himself for me."
Gal. 2:20

St. Paul's words contain the secret of the true life of faith. Here we see the great work that faith has to accomplish in us and for us, in order to allow the living Lord to work His will in us. Christ will accomplish the work in our hearts. The child of God needs time for meditation and adoration, so that the Spirit of God may reveal to Him how completely He will fill our being, accomplishing the work in us.

The Ever—Abiding Spirit

*"The Father shall give you
another Comforter, that He may
be with you forever ... He abideth
with you, and shall be in you."*
John 14:16-17

Read the text over again, and you will see that Christ abiding in us and our abiding in Him – "ye in Me, and I in you" – is altogether dependent upon the indwelling of the Holy Spirit. This can only be done each day as we appear in God's Presence by renewing and confessing our faith in the ever-abiding, indwelling of the Spirit.

CHRIST AND THE SPIRIT

"He that believeth on Me, out of his belly shall flow rivers of living water. This spake He of the Spirit, which they that believed on Him were to receive."
John 7:38-39

Here we learn the important lesson that we must not expect the Holy Spirit always to give us tokens of His Presence. He will ever seek to fix our attention upon Christ. The surest way to be filled with the Spirit is wholeheartedly to occupy ourselves by faith with Christ. We may rely upon the Holy Spirit to enable us to do this.

The Spirit and Christ

"He shall glorify Me; for He shall take of Mine, and shall declare it unto you."
John 16:14

The fullness of the Godhead dwelt in Christ so that Christ as the life of God might dwell in us. All the life and love of God which the Spirit imparts to us is in Christ. Our whole life consists in Union with Christ. As the branch is in the vine, so are we in Christ and He in us. Our first requirement each day is to know that Christ lives in us and that the Holy Spirit will make this an abiding reality. Count on the quiet unseen working of the Holy Spirit in your heart.

CARNAL OR SPIRITUAL?

"And I, brethren, could not speak unto you as unto Spiritual, but as unto carnal, as unto babes in Christ."
1 Cor. 3:1

The difference St. Paul makes between the two kinds of Christians is of great importance. Man's natural life is altogether carnal. The Christian at his new birth receives the Holy Spirit, and immediately there begins a struggle between flesh and spirit. So long as the Christian allows the Spirit to conquer and is led by the Spirit, the power of the Spirit over him increases, and he becomes a spiritual man.

Go on to Perfection

"... let us cease to speak of the first principles of Christ, and press on unto perfection."
Heb. 6:1

Oh, Christian, if hitherto you have been content to know that you have repented and believe in God and so are sure of salvation, I beseech you, do remember this is only the beginning of eternal life. Listen to the call to press on to perfection. This is what God desires and what the Son Himself will do for you. Learn to yield yourself fully to Christ and to find daily in Him the hidden life, so that you may grow in grace and God use you as a soul-winner.

The Building and Its Foundation

*"Let us press on to perfection,
not laying again the foundation
of repentance from dead works,
and of faith toward God."*
Heb. 6:1

That is the life built on the foundation. It is union with the crucified and risen Christ that sets us free from the power of sin, and through the Spirit, Christ Jesus releases us wholly from the power of sin. This life in Christ is the edifice that must be built upon the foundation of Justification.

THE REFORMATION

"For other foundation can no man lay, than that which is laid, which is Jesus Christ; but let each man take heed how he buildeth thereon."
1 Cor. 3:10-11

In the course of centuries the Church of Rome in building had left the true foundation. Instead of justification by faith in Jesus Christ being the foundation of Christian life, the Church itself claimed power to forgive sin. We can never thank God enough for the Reformation when Jesus was proclaimed anew our righteousness – our peace with God.

THE WALK IN CHRIST

"As therefore ye received Christ Jesus the Lord, so walk in Him, rooted and builded up in Him, and stablished in your faith, even as ye were taught, abounding in thanksgiving."
Col. 2:6-7

Let us thank God for the Reformation as a time when the foundation truth of a crucified Savior was laid, but at the same time let us go on to perfection, to a daily uninterrupted walk in Christ wherein we may abound in faith, experiencing the abundance of grace from the fullness there is in Christ for us to enjoy daily.

"THE MEDIATOR OF A NEW COVENANT"

"Ye are come to Jesus the Mediator of a new covenant, and to the blood of sprinkling."
Heb. 12:24

The Mediator is responsible that both sides shall faithfully fulfill the obligations as set forth in the Covenant. Jesus is our surety that God will fulfill His promise. He is surety to God for us that we on our part shall faithfully perform what God requires of us, and He will enable us to keep the Covenant. He also undertook to fulfill the promise.

BETTER PROMISES

"He is the Mediator of a better Covenant, which hath been enacted upon better promises."
Heb. 8:6

Could there be better or more definite promises than these, that God Himself would put His fear into the hearts of His people *so absolutely that they would not depart from Him, and that He would cause them* to keep His judgments and do them? This is the New Covenant of which Jesus is Mediator. Through the Holy Spirit He dwells in us and will keep us from sin, so that we shall have the desire and the power to do God's will in all things.

Fellowship with God

*"That which we have seen
and heard declare we unto
you, that ye also may have
fellowship with us: yea, and
our fellowship is with the Father,
and with His Son Jesus Christ."*
1 John 1:3

Fellowship with God is the unique blessing of the Gospel. If preachers are content to speak only of conversion, forgiveness of sin, and safety after death, they will fail grievously in their work. Christians must be educated to practice the Presence of God, to have fellowship with God, thereby ensuring holy living.

THE FULLNESS OF CHRIST

"And the Word became flesh and dwelt among us ... full of grace and truth. For of His fullness we all received, and grace for grace."
John 1:14, 16

I may receive a purse containing very little or nothing at all, or many golden pounds. There is a great difference between the two! And so with us as Christians. Some receive Christ with the forgiveness of sin and the hope of heaven and know little of the fullness of Christ and all the treasure there is in Him. Other Christians are not satisfied until they can say, "Of His fullness have we received."

THE HEAVENLY LIFE

"Ye died, and your life is hid with Christ in God. Christ is our life."
Col. 3:3-4

When we allow God's Holy Spirit daily to keep alive in us that heavenly life in Christ, we shall grasp what it means to say, "I died with Christ, and I die daily to sin and self and the world in order to make room for that glorious heavenly life that Christ actually lives in me." Then we shall experience, "our conversation is in heaven." Thus shall I have courage to believe that Christ lives in me and reigns and works that which is well pleasing to His Father.

A Royal Priesthood

*"Ye are an elect race, a
royal priesthood."*
1 Peter 2:9

One of the chief reasons for the feeble life in the Church is the mistaken idea that man's happiness is the main object of God's grace. A fatal error! God's aim is far holier and far higher. He saves us on purpose that we in turn shall carry out His purpose in saving others. Each believer is appointed to be the means of imparting to others the new life received in Christ. A royal priesthood! The priestly heart is above all things a sympathetic heart in which the love of Christ constrains us to win souls for Him.

"Apart from Me — Nothing"

*"He that abideth in Me, and I in him,
the same beareth much fruit, for
apart from Me ye can do nothing."*
John 15:5

The Lord Jesus follows His great promise that those who abide in Him will bear much fruit, with the words, "apart from Me, ye can do nothing." What a cause for humiliation! Because the nature we inherit from Adam is so corrupt that in us – that is, in our flesh – dwelleth no good thing. Nay, more, our flesh is at enmity against God. We are under the power of sin to such an extent that we are unable to do anything well-pleasing to God.

The Thrice—Holy God

*"The God of peace Himself
sanctify you wholly ..."*
1 Thess. 5:23

How does the Thrice-holy God accomplish this
great work of sanctifying us wholly? Through
His continual indwelling and fellowship and
breathing of His holy life into us. As upon a cold
day a man may warm himself by standing in the
rays of the sun until its warmth penetrates his
body, so the soul who takes time for communion with God becomes permeated with the
strength of the Triune Holiness.

"The Spirit of His Son"

"Because ye are sons, God sent forth the Spirit of His Son into our hearts, crying, Abba, Father."
Gal. 4:6

The Spirit that dwells in you, O child of God, is none less than the same Spirit that was in Christ, the Spirit of God's holiness. In Gethsemane He taught Christ to cry, "Abba, Father, Thy Will be done." I may also rely upon Him as the Spirit of God's Son to reveal Christ in my heart and always to keep alive in me Christ's life. All that Christ has said of His abiding in me and I in Him, the Spirit of Christ will work in me.

"YE ARE BOUGHT WITH A PRICE"

"... your body is a temple of the Holy Spirit ... and ye are not your own; for ye are bought with a price: glorify God, therefore, in your body."
1 Cor. 6:19-20

What does the Spirit expect of me? Your body is His temple. The temple of God is holy, devoted to His service. You are not your own, you have no right to please yourself. You have been dearly bought with the blood of Christ. The Spirit has absolute right to your whole life. Therefore you must glorify God in your body and your spirit.

Revival

"Turn us again, O Lord God of Hosts. Cause Thy face to shine, and we shall be saved."
Ps. 80:19

Where must the Revival begin? *With God's children*, who may offer themselves to God as instruments to be used by the Holy Spirit, separating themselves from sin, and devoting themselves to the work of saving souls. Christians must realize and prove that the object of their life is God's service and the saving of those for whom Christ shed His blood.

DECEMBER

A Threefold Cord

"All things whatsoever ye pray and ask for, believe that ye have received them, and ye shall have them."
Mark 11:24

To know, To feel, To will, these are the three chief activities of the soul. These three words will show us the way to participate in the fullness of Christ. *To know* – We must not be content with our own thoughts about growth in grace. *To desire* – To desire with our whole heart that for which we pray and be willing to pay the price for it. *To will* – Only by firmness will faith have courage.

THE VINE AND THE BRANCHES

*"He that abideth in Me, and I in him,
the same beareth much fruit."*
John 15:5

In this parable we see what the new life is which the Lord promised His disciples for the work of the Holy Spirit. It clearly mirrors the life of faith.

1. The one object of the life of faith is to bear "much fruit" to the glory of God the Father.

2. The indispensable "cleansing" through the Word that is sharper than a two-edged sword (v. 2).

3. "Abide in Me": Intimate, continuous fellowship.

GIVE TIME TO GOD

"To everything there is a season, and a time to every purpose under the sun."
Eccl. 3:1

This is literally true, there is a time for everything. Can it be true, as so many maintain, that there is no time for communion with God? Is not the most important matter, for which we must find time, fellowship with God in which we may experience His love and His power? Give God time, I beseech you. You need time to feed upon the Word of God and to draw from it life for your soul. Through His Word, His thoughts and His grace enter our hearts and lives.

DEEPER LIFE

"And others fell upon the rocky places, where they had not much earth: and straightway they sprang up, because they had no deepness of earth."
Matt. 13:5

The seed sown upon the rocky places where the soil was superficial sprang up quickly, but it withered as quickly because there was no deepness of earth. We have here a striking picture of so much religion which begins well but which does not endure. The Christian needs a deeper life. Let your whole life be an entrance into that love which passeth knowledge.

Soul—Winning

*"He that abideth in Me, and I
in him, beareth much fruit, for
apart from Me ye can do nothing ...
Herein is My Father glorified,
that ye bear much fruit."*
John 15:5, 8

Fruit is that which a tree or a vine yields for the benefit of its owner. Even so, all that the Lord Jesus has taught us about His abiding in us and we in Him is to make us understand that it is not for our benefit but for His good pleasure and the honor of the Father. We, as branches of the Heavenly Vine, receive and enjoy such astounding grace that we may win souls for Him.

INTERCESSION

"If a man see his brother sinning, he shall ask, and God will give him life."
1 John 5:16

Remember, that you are a branch of the Heavenly Vine not only for your own salvation, but that you may bear much fruit in the conversion of souls. It is as an intercessor that grace is granted you to pray for others, believing assuredly that God will answer you. Think of the change that would come over a community if every believer in it would take time to pray for those who do not believe. How God would be glorified in our bearing much fruit!

CHRIST OUR LIFE

"Ye died, and your life is hid with Christ in God. ... Christ is our life ."
Col. 3:3-4

Only God's Spirit can enable the believer to grasp and appropriate the truth that he was actually crucified and died with Christ. The new life he receives in Christ through the Spirit is life out of death. What joy to know that the new life of God's children around me is also hid with Christ in God! What a bond of union this will be. How sincerely we should love each other and pray for each other. "Your life is hid with Christ in God ... Christ is our life."

The Throne of Grace

"Unto Him that sitteth on the Throne, and unto the Lamb, be the blessing, and the honor, and the glory, and the dominion, forever and ever."
Rev. 5:13

The Throne of Grace, the Throne of God and of the Lamb. The threefold song is the heavenly chorus which was sung at the dedication of the Throne of Grace to the glory of God and of the Lamb. O my soul, bow down and worship and adore. When you draw near to the Throne of Grace, think of what it cost Christ to found that Throne, and what assurance it gives that you will find grace to help in time of need.

THE LAMB IN THE MIDST OF THE THRONE

*"Having then a great High Priest ...
Jesus the Son of God ... Let us
draw near with boldness unto
the Throne of Grace."*
Heb. 4:14-16

The holy God has done His utmost to draw us to Himself and grant us heavenly boldness to pray with the assurance that our defective prayers, through the Lamb on the Throne, the sympathizing High Priest, will be heard and find acceptance with God the Father. O, take time with the vision of the Lamb on the Throne.

Abundant Grace

*"The grace of our Lord abounded
exceedingly with faith and love
which is in Christ Jesus."*
1 Tim. 1:14

What treasures are contained in these words!
Let the Holy Spirit write them in your heart, that
you may receive the full impression of the
"exceeding riches" and the abundance of the
glory of the grace to be received at the Throne
of Grace. Let the thought take possession of you
that all day long the abundance of grace will be
granted to the soul who approaches with boldness and is ready to receive from the sympathizing High Priest that which He has to bestow.

"With All Thy Heart"

*"Thou shalt love the Lord thy
God with all thy heart, and with
all thy soul, and with all thy mind,
and with all thy strength."*
Mark 12:30

Think what it would mean in your prayer-life if
you were strengthened with all might to call
upon God each day! Take this commandment
into your heart and make it the rule of your life
and try to realize that God must have all. It will
make a great difference in your life, and you will
go from strength to strength until you appear
before God in Zion.

THE LAMB AND MISSIONARY WORK

*"Thou wast slain, and didst pur-
chase unto God with Thy blood
men of every tribe, and tongue,
and people, and nation."*
Rev. 5:9

In the Song of the Lamb we find this twofold truth – the Lamb upon the Throne has brought salvation to all the nations and tribes of the earth, and to the Church of the Lamb has been entrusted the distribution of the salvation by the power of the Holy Spirit. Unspeakably glorious is the task of the Missionary!

The Lamb and His Worshipers

*"And hast made us unto our
God kings and priests: and we
shall reign on the earth."*
Rev. 5:10

Let all who read this take to heart the great thought: I come to the Throne of Grace, not only to receive the abundant grace for my own needs, but to be strengthened and fitted for taking that grace to others. The Throne of Grace will become more precious to us as we understand that abundant grace will work within us in greater power when we give our lives to make this salvation known to others.

The Lamb and the Spirit

"I saw ... a Lamb standing ... having seven horns, and seven eyes, which are the seven Spirits of God ..."
Rev. 5:6

Let us learn two great lessons. The first, that the Lamb on the Throne has power to fill us with the Holy Spirit and enable us to follow Him fully and so fit us to commune with God in the power of the blood and be more than conquerors. The second, that it is only through the Spirit that we shall understand the glory of the Lamb and be filled with His love and so stand firm in the faith of that which He can do in us and for us and through us.

The Lamb and Prayer

*"The four-and-twenty elders fell
down before the Lamb, having
each one a harp, and golden
bowls full of incense, which
are the prayers of the saints."*
Rev. 5:8

Remember this. You do not pray alone. All over the world God's children are praying. When with perseverance and faith they entrust their prayers to the Lamb, then in His own time God will graciously send the answer. The wonderful truth that is here revealed is that *the Lamb on the Throne keeps our prayers in safety* to lay them before the Father at the right time.

"THE BLOOD OF THE LAMB"

"They have washed their robes, and made them white in the blood of the lamb. Therefore are they before the Throne of God, and they serve Him day and night in His temple."
Rev. 7:14-15

O Christian, just as you are clothed in suitable garments to meet royalty, so you must each day put on the white robe which has been washed in the blood of the Lamb. You then become one of the royal priesthood who serve God and intercede for souls and for the whole world. The precious blood of Christ gives us access with boldness into God's presence.

FOLLOWING THE LAMB

"These are they which follow the Lamb whithersoever He goeth ..."
Rev. 14:4

The Lamb on the Throne is my Advocate with the Father, who liveth to intercede for me. The Lamb on the Throne has power to lead me and fashion me according to His own image. The Lamb on the throne of my heart is willing and able to increase His own meekness and self-sacrifice within me, and His love to the Father and His redeemed ones. Follow the Lamb! Let this be our watchword and prayer each day!

THE VICTORY OF THE LAMB

"They overcame him [the old serpent, the devil], because of the blood of the Lamb, and because of the word of their testimony; and they loved not their life even unto death."
Rev. 12:11

Dear children of God, if you would in the end be crowned as conquerors in life, be faithful followers of the Lamb. Live as He did. Let your trust in the wonderful life-giving power of the blood and the remembrance of all that He has done for you, be joined to the intense feeling that reckons even life not too precious to be offered up wholly for Him.

THE MARRIAGE OF THE LAMB

*"And He saith unto me, Write,
Blessed are they which are bidden to
the marriage supper of the Lamb."*
Rev. 19:9

All who rejoice in Salvation are called to the marriage of the Lamb, not merely as spectators, but unitedly they form the bride of the Lamb. O child of God, if you really cherish the joyful hope of sitting at the marriage feast of the Lamb, will you not each day make use of the unspeakable privilege of approaching the Throne of Grace? Will you not pray for grace that each day the way may be made more ready for the great heavenly marriage feast of the Lamb?

The Throne of God and of the Lamb

"He showed me a river of water of life, bright as crystal, proceeding out of the Throne of God and of the Lamb."
Rev. 22:1

What does the river of water of life signify? Nothing less than the Holy Spirit which was not given until the Lamb was in the midst of the Throne. Where does the river of the water of life flow? Through the whole earth. It gives us according to our faith and desire that which Christ has promised.

THE HEAVENLY LIFE

"The Throne of God and of the Lamb shall be therein: and His servants shall do Him service; and they shall see His face; and His name shall be on their foreheads."
Rev. 22:3-4

Dear Christian, it is a great thing to approach the Throne of Grace and to receive grace for each day. But there is a still greater blessing when the face of God and of the Lamb are revealed to our earnest gaze, and we walk each day in their light. When the Name of Christ is engraved upon our hearts and upon our foreheads, then we are changed into His image.

The Reign of Grace

"They that receive the abundance of grace shall reign in life through Jesus Christ."
Rom. 5:17

Salvation does not, as many think, mean a life of falling and rising again. No, it is God's will that His children should be conquerors in their life here upon earth. But on one condition – that they should day by day live in the abundance of grace that is to be obtained at the Throne of Grace. Do you not see how everything depends on appearing daily before the Throne of Grace with a deep sense of need but fully assured that abundant grace will be given us?

PENIEL: FACE TO FACE

*"I have seen God face to face,
and my life is preserved."*
Gen. 32:30

In these words of Jacob uttered after he had become Israel, a Prince with God, we find expression of that which prayer meant to him. The words show us what each child of God, through the grace of God and the power of the Holy Spirit, may experience each day. God will cause His face to shine upon us; *we shall see Him face to face* and be delivered. Persevering prayer is needed to bring the soul into the steadfast conviction that God will really make Himself known.

"I Am the Lord, and There Is None Else"

"Jesus answered, The first of all the commandments is: Hear, O Israel! The Lord our God, the Lord is One."
Mark 12:29

The law may command us to love, but it cannot make us love. It is powerless to force us to love God. Love can be called forth only by that which is worthy of love. Love to God can be born only of the knowledge of Him as the one true God in His excellent greatness and glory, His unspeakable love and compassion. Dear reader, here you have the secret of the prayer-life – to meet God each day.

THE ABIDING PRESENCE OF GOD

*"The Lord is nigh unto all them
that call upon Him, to all that
call upon Him in truth."*
Ps. 145:18

You long to experience continually the nearness of God. Here is the secret: Pray, pray without ceasing. Then you will have the assurance: "The Lord is nigh unto all who call upon Him." Prayer has a wonderful power of helping us to draw near to God and keeping us in His presence. God is everywhere and as the Almighty One is ever ready and able to grant us unbroken fellowship with Him.

Take Time with God

"To everything there is a season, and a time to every purpose under the heaven."
Eccl. 3:1

Everything on earth needs time. Think of the hours per day for so many years that a child spends at school gathering the rudiments of knowledge that he may cope with this life. How much longer then should we spend in learning from God for life everlasting? O Christian, give the holy, gracious God all the time you can until His light and life and love fill your whole life and you abide in Christ and His love through His Word and through prayer.

THE WILL

"All Judah rejoiced, for they had sought Him with their whole desire; and He was found of them."
2 Chron. 15:15

The will is the royal faculty of the soul; it rules over the whole man. Many people become the slaves of sin because they do not decide with a firm will to listen to the voice of conscience. Many Christians make no advance in the prayer-life because they have not the courage to say with a strong purpose of will: "By God's help I will do all that God's Word and my own conscience bid me do. I will make time for prayer and quiet fellowship with Him."

CHRIST'S LOVE TO US

*"A new commandment I give
unto you, That ye love one another,
even as I have loved you."*
John 13:34

We are ever ready to say: "We cannot love others as Christ has loved us." It is not impossible. The Holy Spirit, as the power of this holy love, *sheds it abroad in our hearts*. This is God's own Word. He who meditates on it *until he believes it* will have courage to bring his petitions to the Throne of Grace and to receive the love which passes all understanding.

OUR LOVE TO CHRIST

"If ye love Me, ye will keep My commandments."
John 14:15

The Father and the Son dwell in the hearts of those who love Jesus and keep His commandments. Such can say with St. Paul, "Christ lives in me," and will love the brethren and all around them with the love wherewith God loved His Son. Dear Christian, as Christ loved you and you abide in His love, you will be enabled to keep His commandments. The measure of His sacrifice for you will be the measure of your willing surrender to Him in all things.

Our Love to the Brethren

*"This is My commandment,
that ye love one another, even
as I have loved you."*
John 15:12

Let us try to understand what the Lord really means by this command. He came to earth to make known God's love to us. He was returning to the Father. He had revealed the love of God the Father and would leave this love on earth in charge of His disciples. He said to them: "Love one another, as I have loved you. Remember that through the Holy Spirit, whom I will send, I am dwelling within you and will enable you to love the brethren with My own love."

LOVE DEMANDS ALL

"Hereby know we love, because He laid down His life for us; and we ought to lay down our lives for the brethren."
1 John 3:16

Try to grasp this truth. The strength of God's love in Christ enabled Him to give up His life wholly for us. The same strength is available for us, and as we yield ourselves wholly to it, we shall be able to make the welfare of souls the central object of our lives. One who gives himself wholly into the keeping of God's love will feel its power and all-sufficiency. This is the blessedness of the Christian life.

D1409659

TEMPERATE IN ALL THINGS

*"Every man that striveth in
the games exerciseth
self-control in all things ... "*
1 Cor. 9:25 R.V.

Paul here reminds us of the well-known principle that anyone competing in the public games is "temperate in all things". Everything, however attractive, that might be a hindrance in the race is given up in order to obtain an earthly prize. And we who strive for an incorruptible crown and that Christ may be Lord of all – shall we not be temperate in all things that could in the very least prevent our following the Lord Jesus with an undivided heart?

The Dying of the Lord Jesus

"Always bearing about in the body the dying of Jesus, that the life also of Jesus may be manifested in our body ... So then death worketh in us, but life in you."
2 Cor. 4:10, 12

If we are indeed to live for the welfare of others around us, and sacrifice our ease and pleasure to win souls for our Lord, it will be true of us as of Paul, that we are able to say: Death worketh in us, but life in those for whom we pray and labor. It is in the fellowship of the sufferings of Christ that the crucified Lord can live out and work out His life in us and through us.

THE CROSS AND THE SPIRIT

"How much more shall the blood of Christ, who through the Eternal Spirit offered Himself without blemish unto God, cleanse your conscience?"
Heb. 9:14 R.V.

Have we not here the reason that our prayers for the mighty working of the Holy Spirit are not more abundantly answered? We have prayed too little that the Holy Spirit might glorify Christ in us in the fellowship and the conformity to His sufferings. The Spirit, who led Christ to the cross, is longing and is able to maintain in us the life of abiding in the crucified Jesus.

The Veil Of The Flesh

*"Having therefore, brethren, bold-
ness to enter into the holy place
by the blood of Jesus, by the way
which He dedicated for us, a new
and living way, through the veil,
that is to say, His flesh."*
Heb. 10:19-20

Have we not here the reason why many Christians can never attain to close fellowship with
God? They have never yielded the flesh as an
accursed thing to the condemnation of the
cross. They desire to enter into the holiest of all
and yet allow the flesh with its desires and
pleasures to rule over them.

GOD'S BEST SECRETS

© 1995: Christian Art, P.O. Box 1599, Vereeniging, South Africa

ISBN 1-86852-053-6

Material in this book is adapted from *GOD'S BEST SECRETS* by Andrew Murray.
Edited by J. Sandenberg from original manuscript

Printed in Singapore.

JANUARY

From Day to Day

*"The inner man is renewed
from day to day."*
2 Cor. 4:16

The Lord Jesus will every day from heaven continue His work in me. But on one condition – *the soul must give Him time each day* to impart His love and His grace. Time alone with the Lord Jesus each day is the indispensable condition of growth and power.

FELLOWSHIP WITH GOD

*"He that loveth Me shall be loved
of my Father. I will love Him."*
John 14:21

Our relationship to Christ rests on His deep,
tender love to us. We are not able of ourselves
to render Him this love. But the Holy Spirit will
do the work in us. For this we need to separate
ourselves each day from the world and turn in
faith to the Lord Jesus, that He may shed abroad
His love in our hearts, *so that we may be filled
with a great love to Him.*

JESUS

*"Thou shalt call His Name Jesus,
for He shall save His people
from their sins."*
Matt. 1:21

It is *through personal fellowship* with Him that Jesus saves us from our sins. As you learn to go apart with Him alone each day, you will experience His presence with you, enabling you all through the day to love Him, to serve Him, and to walk in His ways.

The Inner Chamber

*"When thou prayest enter
into thine inner chamber."*
Matt. 6:6, R.V.

"Enter into thine inner chamber, and having shut thy door, pray to thy Father which is in secret." That means two things. Shut the world out, withdraw from all worldly thoughts and occupations, and shut yourself in alone with God to pray to Him in secret. *Prayer in fellowship* with Jesus cannot be in vain.

Faith

"Only believe."
Mark 5:36

We must have *faith in all that God is willing to do for us*. We must have faith each day according to our special needs. God is infinitely great and powerful; Christ has so much grace for each new day that our faith must reach out afresh each day according to the need of the day.

THE WORD OF GOD

"Man shall not live by bread alone, but by every word that proceedeth out of the mouth of God."
Matt. 4:4

To secure a strong and powerful spiritual life, God's Word every day is indispensable. And if you seek fellowship with Him, you will find Him in His Word. Christ will teach you to commune with the Father through the Word, even as was His custom.

How to Read God's Word

*"Blessed is the man whose
delight is in the law of the Lord,
and in His law doth he meditate day and night."*
Ps. 1:1-2

*R*ead with the expectation of the guidance of
God's Spirit. It is God's Spirit alone that can
make the Word a living power in our hearts and
lives. As you read, remember that God's Word
and God's Spirit are inseparable. *Read with the
firm purpose of keeping the Word day and night
in your heart and in your life.*

THE WORD AND PRAYER

*"Quicken Me, O Lord,
according to Thy Word."*
Ps. 119:107

The Word teaches me how to pray – with strong desire, with a firm faith, and with constant perseverance. The Word teaches me not only what I am, but what I may become through God's grace. O Christian, learn this great lesson, *to renew your strength each day in God's Word, and so pray according to His will.*

OBEDIENCE

*"Obey My voice ... and I
will be your God."*
Jer. 11:4

Pray God to imprint this lesson on your heart:
the life of faith is a life of obedience. As Christ
lived in obedience to the Father, so we too
need obedience for a life in the love of God.
Faith can firmly trust Christ to enable us to
live such a life of love and of obedience.

Confession of Sin

"If we confess our sins, He is faithful and just to forgive us our sins, and to cleanse us from all unrighteousness."
1 John 1:9

Confession means not only that I confess my sin with shame but that I hand it over to God, trusting Him to take it away. By an act of faith I reckon on God to deliver me. This deliverance means, in the first place, that I know my sins are forgiven, and secondly, that Christ undertakes to cleanse me from the sin and keep me from its power.

THE FIRST LOVE

*"I have somewhat against
thee, because thou hast
left thy first love."*
Rev. 2:4

This is a thought of great significance – a church or a community or a Christian may be an example in every good work, and yet – *the tender love to the Lord Jesus in the inner chamber is missing. His love can be satisfied with nothing less than a deep, personal love on our part.*

THE HOLY SPIRIT

"He shall glorify Me; for He shall receive of Mine, and show it unto you."
John 16:14

When once we have grasped this truth, we will begin to feel our deep dependence on the Holy Spirit and pray the Father to send Him in power into our hearts. The Spirit will teach us to love the Word, to meditate on it, and to keep it. He will reveal the love of Christ to us, that we may love Him with a pure heart fervently.

CHRIST'S LOVE TO US

*"Even as the Father hath loved
Me, I also have loved you:
abide ye in My love."*
John 15:9 R.V.

Of what value is abundance of riches if love is lacking between husband and wife or parents and children? And in our religion, of what value is all knowledge and zeal in God's work without the knowledge and experience of Christ's love? He yearns that this everlasting love should rest upon us and work within us, that we may abide in it day by day.

Our Love to Christ

"Jesus Christ, whom not having seen, ye love: in whom though now ye see Him not, yet believing, ... "
1 Peter 1:8 R.V.

What a wonderful description of the Christian life! People who had never seen Christ yet truly loved Him and believed on Him, so that their hearts were filled with unspeakable joy. Such is the life of Christians who really love their Lord.

LOVE TO THE BRETHREN

"A new commandment I give unto you, that ye love one another, even as I have loved you, that ye also love one another."
John 13:34; 15:12

If we exhibit the love that was in God toward Christ and in Christ to us, the world will be obliged to confess that our Christianity is genuine and from above. Pray that you may love your fellow-believers with the same love with which Christ loved you.

Love to Souls

"Know that he which converteth a sinner from the error of this way, shall save a soul from death."
James 5:20

What a wonderful thought – that I may save a soul from everlasting death. How can this be? If I convert him from the error of his ways. This is the calling not only of the minister, but of every Christian – to work for the salvation of sinners.

THE SPIRIT OF LOVE

*"The love of God is shed abroad in
our hearts, by the Holy Spirit,
which is given unto us."*
Rom. 5:5

We need continually to remind ourselves that
it is not in our own strength or even by serious
thought that we can attain to the love of Christ.
It is only as we are wholly surrendered to the
leading of the Spirit that we will be able to live
according to God's will. Unless you wait upon
God daily on your knees for His Spirit to be
revealed in your heart, you cannot live in this
love.

PERSEVERING PRAYER

"Pray without ceasing."
1 Thess. 5:17

"Pray without ceasing." You will find it an unspeakable blessing to do so. You will ask whether your prayer is really in accordance with the will of God and the Word of God. You will inquire if it is in the right spirit and in the Name of Christ. Keep on praying – you will learn that the delay in the answer to prayer is one of the most precious means of grace that God can bestow on you.

THE PRAYER MEETING

"These all continued with one accord in prayer and supplication." "And they were all filled with the Holy Ghost."
Acts 1:14; 2:4

God's children meet together to lift up their hearts unitedly to God. By this means Christians are drawn closer to each other. Those who are weak are strengthened and encouraged by the testimony of the older and more experienced members, and even young Christians have the opportunity of telling of the joy of the Lord.

INTERCESSION

*"Praying at all seasons in the Spirit
... in all perseverance and
supplication for all the saints."*
Eph. 6:18

Christian, begin to use intercession as a means of grace for yourself and for others. If you surrender yourself to the guidance of the Holy Spirit and live a life wholly for God, you will realize that the time spent in prayer is an offering well-pleasing to God, bringing blessing to yourself and power into the lives of those for whom you pray.

Prayer and Fasting

*"And Jesus said unto them,
'Because of your unbelief ...
this kind goeth not out but
by prayer and fasting.'"*
Matt. 17:20-21

Our Lord here teaches us that a life of faith requires both prayer and fasting. That is, prayer grasps the power of heaven, fasting loosens the hold on earthly pleasure. For the real practice of prayer and taking hold of God and having communion with Him, it is necessary that all that can please the flesh must be sacrificed.

The Spirit of Prayer

*"The Spirit maketh inter-
cession for the saints."*
Rom. 8:27

I may bow in silence before God in the confidence that His Holy Spirit will teach me to pray. The Spirit is the Spirit of prayer. It is not my work but God's work in me. As we think of this, our attitude should be one of silent expectation that as we pray, the Holy Spirit may help our infirmities and pray within us with groanings that cannot be uttered.

Wholly for Christ

"One died for all ... that they which live should no longer live unto themselves, but unto Him ... "
2 Cor. 5:14-15 R.V.

Pray for grace to live wholly for God in seeking souls and in serving His people. Take time from day to day to be so united to Christ in the inner man that you can say with all your heart: I live wholly for Him who gave Himself wholly for me and now lives in heaven wholly for me.

THE CROSS OF CHRIST

"I am crucified with Christ."
Gal. 2:20

The Christian shares with Christ in the cross. He lives as one who has died with Christ. This is a deep spiritual truth. Think and pray over it, and the Holy Spirit will teach you. The power of His death will work in you, and you will become like Him in His death, and you will know Him and the power of His resurrection.

THE WORLD

"Love not the world, neither the things that are in the world. If any man love the world, the love of the Father is not in him."
1 John 2:15

Christian, you live in a dangerous world. Cleave fast to the Lord Jesus. As He teaches you to shun the world and its attractions, your love will go out to Him in loyal-hearted service. But remember – There must be daily fellowship with Jesus. His love alone can expel the love of the world. Take time to be alone with your Lord.

Put on Christ

"Put ye on the Lord Jesus Christ, and make not provision for the flesh, to fulfill the lusts thereof."
Rom. 13:14

"Put on the Lord Jesus." Not alone at conversion, but from day to day. As my garments cover me and protect me from wind and sun, even so Christ Jesus will be my beauty, my defense, and my joy. As I commune with Him in prayer, He imparts Himself to me and strengthens me to walk as one who is in Him and bound to Him forever.

The Strength Of The Christian

*"Finally, my brethren, be strong
in the Lord, and in the power
of His might."*
Eph. 6:10

Pray for God's Spirit to enlighten your eyes.
Believe in the divine power working within
you. Pray that the Holy Spirit may reveal it to
you and appropriate the promise that God will
manifest His Power in your heart, supplying all
your needs.

The Whole Heart

*"With my whole heart
have I sought Thee."*
Ps. 119:10

Think over it. Pray over it. Speak it out before God until you feel: I really mean what I say, and I have the assurance that God will hear my prayer. Say it each morning as you approach God in prayer: I seek Thee with my whole heart.

In Christ

"Of God are ye in Christ Jesus."
1 Cor. 1:30

Let our faith take hold of the words: "It is God that stablisheth us in Christ." "Of God I am in Christ Jesus." The Holy Spirit will make it our experience. Pray earnestly and follow the leading of the Spirit. The word will take root in your heart, and you will realize something of its heavenly power.

CHRIST IN ME

*"Know ye not ... that
Jesus Christ is in you?"*
2 Cor. 13:5

What a difference it would make in our lives if we could take time every morning to be filled with the thought: Christ is in me. But this knowledge does not come easily. Through faith in God's Word, the Christian accepts it, and the Holy Spirit will lead us into all truth. Take time this very day to realize and appropriate this blessing in prayer.

CHRIST IS ALL

"Christ is all and in all."
Col. 3:11

In the eternal counsel of God, in the redemption on the cross, as King on the throne in heaven and on earth – *Christ is all!* In the salvation of sinners, in their justification and sanctification, *Christ is all!* God be praised to all eternity: Christ, my Christ, is my all in all!

FEBRUARY

INTERCESSION

"Pray one for another."
James 5:16

What a mystery of glory there is in prayer! On the one hand, we see God, in His holiness and love and power, waiting, longing to bless man; and on the other, sinful man, a worm of the dust, bringing down from God by prayer the very life and love of heaven to dwell in his heart.

THE OPENING OF THE EYES

"And Elisha prayed and said: Lord, open his eyes, that he may see ..."
2 Kings 6:17

How wonderfully the prayer of Elisha for his servant was answered! The young man saw the mountain full of chariots of fire and horsemen about Elisha. How little the children of God live in the faith of that heavenly vision – the power of the Holy Spirit on them, with them, and in them for their own spiritual life and as their strength joyfully to witness for their Lord and His work!

MAN'S PLACE IN GOD'S PLAN

"The heaven, even the heavens, are the Lord's; but the earth hath He given to the children of men."
Ps. 115:16

The work God had begun and prepared was by man to be carried out in fulfillment of God's purpose. And so nature teaches us the wonderful partnership to which God calls man for the carrying out of the work of creation to its destined end.

Intercession in the Plan of Redemption

"O Thou that hears prayer, unto Thee shall all flesh come."
Ps. 65:2

When God made the plan of redemption, His object was to restore man to the place from which he had fallen. God regards intercession as the highest expression of His people's readiness to receive and to yield themselves wholly to the working of His almighty power.

God Seeks Intercessors

*"He saw that there was no man,
and wondered that there
was no intercessor."*
Isa. 59:16

God rules the world and His Church through the prayers of His people. "That God should have made the extension of His Kingdom to such a large extent dependent on the faithfulness of His people in prayer is a stupendous mystery and yet an absolute certainty." God calls for intercessors; in His grace He has made His work dependent on them; He waits for them.

CHRIST AS INTERCESSOR

*"He is able to save them to the
uttermost that come unto God by
Him, seeing He ever liveth to
make intercession for them."*
Heb. 7:25

In His life on earth Christ began His work as
Intercessor. Think of His words to Peter, "I
have prayed for thee, that thy faith fail not."
Now that He is seated at God's right hand, He
continues, as our great High Priest, the work of
intercession without ceasing. But with this
difference, *that He gives His people power to
take part in it.*

The Intercessors God Seeks

"I have set watchmen upon Thy walls, O Jerusalem; they shall never hold their peace day nor night: ye that are the Lord's remembrancers, take ye no rest and give Him no rest."
Isa. 62:6-7

If ever there was a time when God's elect should cry day and night to Him, it is now. Will you not, dear reader, offer yourself to God for this blessed work of intercession and learn to count it the highest privilege of your life to be a channel through whose prayers God's blessing can be brought down to earth?

THE SCHOOL OF INTERCESSION

*"Who in the days of His flesh,
when He had offered up prayers
and supplications with strong
crying and tears, ..."*
Heb. 5:7

Christ, as Head, is Intercessor in heaven; we, as the members of His Body, are partners with Him on earth. Intercession must not be a passing interest; it must become an ever-growing object of intense desire for which above everything we long and live. It is the life of consecration and self-sacrifice that will indeed give power for intercession.

THE NAME OF JESUS: THE POWER OF INTERCESSION

"Hitherto have ye asked nothing in My name. At that day ye shall ask in My name; ask and ye shall receive, that your joy may be full."
John 16:24, 26

When our Lord Jesus in His farewell discourse gave His unlimited prayer promise, He sent the disciples out into the world with this consciousness: "He who sits upon the throne and who lives in my heart has promised that what I ask in His name I shall receive. *He will do it.*"

Prayer: The Work
of the Spirit

*"God has sent forth the Spirit
of His Son into your hearts,
crying, 'Abba, Father.'"*
Gal. 4:6

*The Holy Spirit of Jesus is actually given into
our hearts* that we may pray in His likeness, in
His name, and in His power. It is the Christian
who is wholly yielded to the leading of the Holy
Spirit who will feel urged by the compulsion of
a Divine love to the undivided surrender to a
life of continual intercession, because he knows
that it is God who is working in him.

JESUS CHRIST: OUR EXAMPLE IN INTERCESSION

"He bare the sin of many and made intercession for the transgressors."
Isa. 53:12

The Lord Jesus has in very deed taken us up into a partnership with Himself in carrying out the great work of intercession. He in heaven and we on earth must have one mind, one aim in life – that we should, from love to the Father and to the lost, consecrate our lives to intercession for God's blessing.

God's Will and Ours

"Thy will be done."
Matt. 26:42

As in God so in man, desire is the great moving power. And just as man had yielded himself to a life of desire after the things of the earth and the flesh, God had to redeem him and to educate him into a life of harmony with Himself. His one aim was that man's desire should be in perfect accord with His own.

THE BLESSEDNESS OF A LIFE OF INTERCESSION

*"..., take ye no rest and give
Him no rest, till He make
Jerusalem a praise in the earth."*
Isa. 62:6-7

What blessedness, in union with other children of God, to strive together in prayer until the victory is gained over difficulties here on earth or over the powers of darkness in high places! It is worth living for, to know that God will use me as an intercessor to receive and dispense here on earth His heavenly blessing and the power of His Holy Spirit.

THE PLACE OF PRAYER

"These all continued with one accord in prayer and supplication."
Acts 1:14

"Wait for the promise of the Father." Their own duty was to wait in united and unceasing prayer for the power of the Holy Spirit as the gift from on high for their witness to Christ to the ends of the earth. A praying Church, a Spirit-filled Church, a witnessing Church with all the world as its sphere and aim – such is the Church of Jesus Christ.

Paul as an Intercessor

"I bow my knees unto the Father, that He would grant you to be strengthened with might by His Spirit."
Eph. 3:14, 16

The whole relationship between pastor and people is a heavenly one, spiritual and Divine, and can only be maintained by unceasing prayer. It is when ministers and people waken up to the consciousness that the power and blessing of the Holy Spirit is waiting for their united and unceasing prayer that the Church will begin to know something of what Pentecostal Apostolic Christianity is.

INTERCESSION FOR
LABORERS

"... pray ye therefore the Lord of the harvest, that He will send forth laborers into His harvest."
Matt. 9:37-38

Christ meant to teach us that however large the field may be and however few the laborers, prayer is the best, the sure, the only means for supplying the need. The churches all complain of the lack of laborers and of funds. Does not Christ's voice call us to the united and unceasing prayer of the first disciples? God is faithful by the power of His Spirit to supply every need.

INTERCESSION FOR INDIVIDUAL SOULS

"Ye shall be gathered one by one, O ye children of Israel."
Isa. 27:12

Oh, when will Christians learn the great truth that "what God in heaven desires to do *needs prayer on earth as its indispensable condition*." It is as we realize this that we shall see that intercession is the chief element in the conversion of souls. All our efforts are vain without the power of the Holy Spirit given in answer to prayer.

INTERCESSION FOR MINISTERS

"Finally, brethren, pray for us."
2 Thess. 3:1

If Paul, after having preached for twenty years in the power of God, still needed the prayer of the Church, how much more does the ministry in our day need it? Let all intercessors who are seeking to enter more deeply into their blessed work give a larger place to the ministry, whether of their own church or of other churches.

PRAYER FOR ALL SAINTS

*"With all prayer and supplication
praying at all seasons in the
Spirit, ... for all the saints."*
Eph. 6:18 R.V.

The great lack in true believers often is that in prayer they are occupied with themselves and with what God must do for them. It is as we forget ourselves, in the faith that God will take charge of us, and yield ourselves to the great and blessed work of calling down the blessing of God on our brothers and sisters.

MISSIONARY INTERCESSION

*"When they had fasted and prayed,
and laid their hands on them, they
sent them away."*
Acts 13:3

Missions have their root in the love of Christ
that was proved on the cross and now lives in
our hearts. As men are so earnest in seeking to
carry out God's plans for the natural world, so
God's children should be at least as whole-
hearted in seeking to bring Christ's love to
everyone. Intercession is the chief means appointed by God to bring the great redemption
within the reach of all.

THE GRACE OF INTERCESSION

*"Continue in prayer, and watch in
the same with thanksgiving, withal
praying also for us."*
Col. 4:2-3

God delights in nothing so much as in prayer.
Shall we not learn to believe that the highest
blessings of heaven will be unfolded to us as we
pray more?

United Intercession

"There is one body, and one Spirit."
Eph. 4.4

It is only when intercession *for the whole Church, by the whole Church* ascends to God's throne that the Spirit of unity and of power can have its full sway. *It is in the cultivation and increase of the Spirit and in the exercise of intercession that the true unity can be realized.*

UNCEASING INTERCESSION

"Pray without ceasing."
1 Thess. 5:17

"Pray without ceasing," is simply a needless and impossible life of perfection. Who can do it? We can get to heaven without it. To the true believer, on the contrary, it holds out the promise of the highest happiness, of a life crowned by all the blessings that can be brought down on souls through his intercession.

INTERCESSION: THE LINK BETWEEN HEAVEN AND EARTH

"Thy will be done, as in heaven, so on earth."
Luke 11:2

The intercession of the Son begun upon earth, continued in heaven, and carried on by His redeemed people upon earth, will bring about the mighty change: "As in heaven, so on earth." Every prayer of a parent for a child, of a believer for the saving of the lost, or for more grace to those who have been saved is part of the great unceasing cry going up day and night from this earth, "As in heaven, so on earth."

God's Desires

"Here will I dwell; for I have desired it."
Ps. 132:13-14

Here you have the one great desire of God that moved Him in the work of redemption. His heart longed for man, to dwell with him and in him. As the desire of God toward us fills our hearts, it will waken within us the desire to gather others around us to become His dwelling too.

MAN'S DESIRE

"Delight thyself in the Lord;
and He shall give thee the
desires of thine heart."
Ps. 37:4

"Delight thyself in the Lord," and in His life of love, "and He will give thee the desires of thine heart." We may be sure that, as we delight in what God delights in, such prayer is inspired by God and will have its answer.

My Great Desire

*"... that I may dwell in the house of
the Lord all the days of my life, ..."*
Ps. 27:4

Here we have man's response to God's desire
to dwell in us. When the desire of God toward
us begins to rule the life and heart, our desire
is fixed on one thing and that is to dwell in the
house of the Lord all the days of our life, to
behold the beauty of the Lord, to worship Him
in the beauty of holiness.

INTERCESSION DAY AND NIGHT

"Shall not God avenge His own elect, which cry day and night unto Him, ..."
Luke 18:7

Is such prayer night and day really needed and really possible? Most assuredly, when the heart is first so entirely possessed by the desire that it cannot rest until this is fulfilled. The life has so come under the power of the heavenly blessing that nothing can keep it from sacrificing all to obtain it.

THE HIGH PRIEST AND HIS INTERCESSION

"We have such an High Priest, ... He ever liveth to make intercession for them."
Heb. 7:25-26; 8:1

Our great High Priest. He alone has power with God, in a never-ceasing intercession, to obtain from the Father what His people need. The blessing that He obtains from His Father for us, He holds for His people to receive from Him through their fervent supplication to be dispensed to the souls among whom He has placed them as His witnesses and representatives.

MARCH

A Royal Priesthood

"Call unto Me, and I will answer thee, and show thee great and mighty things which thou knowest not."
Jer. 33:3

Children of God, God counts upon you to take your place before His throne as intercessors. Awake, I pray you, to the consciousness of your holy calling as a royal priesthood. Let each one say whether he is not willing to make intercession the one chief object of his life? Is this asking too much – to yield your life for this holy service of the royal priesthood to that blessed Lord who gave Himself for us?

INTERCESSION: A DIVINE REALITY

"And another angel came, ... and there was given unto him much incense, that he should offer it with the prayers of all saints ..."
Rev. 8:3

Intercession is an essential element in God's redeeming purpose. Christ's intercession in heaven is essential to His carrying out of the work He began upon earth, but He calls for the intercession of the saints in the attainment of His object. As the reconciliation was dependent on Christ's doing His part, so in the accomplishment of the work, He calls on the Church to do her part.

TRUE WORSHIP

"Worship God."
Rev. 22:9

How is one to attain to this nearness to God and fellowship with Him? The answer is simple: *We must give God time to make Himself known to us.* Believe with all your whole heart that just as you present yourself to God as a supplicant, *so God presents Himself to you as the Hearer of prayer.* But you cannot realize this except as you give Him time and quiet. He Himself will give the assurance that in His time your prayer will be heard.

GOD IS A SPIRIT

*"God is a Spirit: ... worship
Him in spirit and in truth."*
John 4:24

God is a Spirit, most holy and most glorious. He gave us a spirit with the one object of *holding fellowship with Himself.* Through sin that power has been darkened and well-nigh quenched. There is no way for its restoration but by presenting the soul in stillness before God for the working of His Holy Spirit in our spirit. Deeper than our thoughts and feelings, God will in our inward part, in our spirits within us, teach us to worship Him in spirit and in truth.

INTERCESSION AND ADORATION

"Worship the Lord in the beauty of holiness."
Ps. 96:9

Intercession will lead to the feeling of the need of a deeper adoration. Adoration will give new power for intercession. A true intercession and a deeper adoration will ever be found to be inseparable. The secret of true adoration can only be known by the soul that gives time to tarry in God's presence and that yields itself to God. "Oh, come let us worship and bow down, let us kneel before the Lord our Maker ..." Give unto the Lord the glory due unto His name."

THE DESIRE FOR GOD

*"With my soul have I
desired Thee in the night."*
Isa. 26:9

What is the chief thing, the greatest and most glorious, that one can see or find upon earth? *Nothing less than God Himself.* And what is the chief and the best and the most glorious thing that one needs every day and can do every day? Nothing less than to seek and to know and to love and to praise this glorious God. As glorious as God is, so is the glory which begins to work in the heart and life of those who give themselves to live for God.

SILENT ADORATION

"My soul is silent unto God ... for my expectation is from Him."
Ps. 62:1, 5

When we in our littleness and God in His glory meet, we all understand that what God says has infinitely more worth than what we say. And yet our prayer so often consists in the utterance *of our thoughts* of what we need, that we give God no time to speak to us. Our prayers are often so indefinite and vague. It is a great lesson to learn that to be silent unto God is the secret of true adoration. Let us remember the promise, "In quietness and confidence shall be your strength."

THE LIGHT OF GOD'S COUNTENANCE

"God is light."
1 John 1:5
"The Lord is my light."
Ps. 27:1

Every morning the sun rises, and we walk in its light and perform our daily duties with gladness. Whether we think of it or not, the light of the sun shines on us all day. Every morning the light of God shines upon His children. But in order to enjoy the light of God's countenance, the soul must turn to God and trust Him to let His light shine upon it.

FAITH IN GOD

*"Jesus said unto them:
'Have faith in God.'"*
Mark 11:22

As the eye is the organ by which we see the light and rejoice in it, so faith is the power by which we see the light of God and walk in it. Let our one desire be to take time and be still before God, believing with an unbounded faith in His longing to make Himself known to us. Let us feed on God's Word to make us strong in faith. Let that faith have large thoughts of what God's glory is; of what His power is to reveal Himself to us; of what His longing love is to get complete possession of us.

ALONE WITH GOD

*"And it came to pass, as
He was alone praying."*
Luke 9:18

We need to be alone with God, to yield to the presence and the power of His holiness, of His life, and of His love. Christ on earth needed it; He could not live the life of a Son here in the flesh without at times separating Himself entirely from His surroundings and being alone with God. How much more must this be indispensable to us! Take time, O my soul, to be alone with God. The time will come when you will be amazed at the thought that one could suggest that five minutes was enough.

WHOLLY FOR GOD

*"... there is none upon earth that
I desire beside Thee."*
Ps. 73:25

Alone with God – This is a word of the deepest
importance. May we seek grace from God to
reach its depths. Then shall we learn that there
is another word of equally deep significance –
Wholly for God. Nature teaches us that if anyone
desires to do a great work, he must give wholly
to it. This law is especially true of the love of a
mother for her child. She gives herself wholly
to the little one whom she loves. And shall we
not think it reasonable that the great God of Love
should have us wholly for Himself?

THE KNOWLEDGE OF GOD

*"This is life eternal, that
they might know Thee."*
John 17:3

The knowledge of God is absolutely necessary for the spiritual life. *It is life eternal.* Not the intellectual knowledge we receive from others or through our own power of thought, but the living, experimental knowledge *in which God makes Himself known to the soul.* Just as the rays of the sun on a cold winter's day warm the body, imparting its heat to us, *so the living God sheds the life-giving rays of His holiness and love into the heart that waits on Him.*

GOD THE FATHER

"Baptizing in the name of the Father, and of the Son, and of the Holy Spirit."
Matt. 28:19

When Christ taught us to say, "Our Father, which art in heaven," He immediately added, "Hallowed be Thy Name." As God is holy, so we are to be holy too. And there is no way of becoming holy but by counting that name most holy and drawing nigh to Him in prayer. How often we speak that name without any sense of the unspeakable privilege of our relation to God. If we would just take time to worship Him in His Father love.

GOD THE SON

*"Grace to you and peace from
God our Father and the
Lord Jesus Christ."*
Rom. 1:7

There may be times when one prays chiefly to God the Father. But it may cause spiritual loss if we do not grasp the truth that it is only through faith in Christ and *in living union with Him* that we can enjoy a full and abiding fellowship with God. Take time to meditate and believe, to expect all from God the Father who sits upon the throne and from the Lord Jesus Christ, the Lamb in the midst of the throne. Then you will learn truly to worship God.

GOD THE HOLY SPIRIT

*"Through Him we both have access
by one Spirit unto the Father."*
Eph. 2:18

In our communion with God in the inner chamber, we must guard against the danger of seeking to know God and Christ in the power of the intellect or the emotions. *The Holy Spirit has been given for the express purpose that "by Him we may have access to the Father through the Son."* Let us beware lest our labor be in vain because we do not wait for the teaching of the Spirit. Be strong in the faith that He is working secretly in you and give yourself wholly to His guidance.

The Secret of the Lord

"Enter into thy closet, and when thou hast shut thy door, pray ... and thy Father which seeth in secret shall reward thee openly."
Matt. 6:6

Christ longed greatly that His disciples should know God as their Father and that they should have secret fellowship with Him. In His own life He found it not only indispensable but the highest happiness to meet the Father in secret. And He would have us realize that it is impossible to be true, wholehearted disciples *without daily communion with the Father in heaven* who waits for us in secret.

Half an Hour Silence in Heaven

"And there was silence in heaven about the space of half an hour."
Rev. 8:1

How often the complaint is heard that there is no time for prayer. Brothers and sisters, God longs to bless you. Is it not worth the trouble to take half an hour alone with God? In heaven itself there was need for half an hour's silence to present the prayers of the saints before God. If you persevere, you may find that the half-hour that seems the most difficult in the whole day may at length become the most blessed in your whole life.

GOD'S GREATNESS

*"Thou art great, and doest wondrous
things; Thou art God alone."*
Ps. 86:10

When we commence an important work, we take time and give our attention to consider the greatness of the undertaking. Yet how superficial is our knowledge of God's greatness. The right comprehension of God's greatness will take time. But if we give God the honor that is His due and if our faith grows strong in the knowledge of what a great and powerful God we have, we shall be drawn to tarry in the inner chamber to bow in humble worship before this great and mighty God.

A Perfect Heart

*"For the eyes of the Lord run to
and fro ... in behalf of them whose
heart is perfect toward Him."*
2 Chron. 16:9

Amazingly, earnest Christians, who attend to their daily work wholeheartedly, are content to take things easy in the service of God. They do not realize that if anywhere, they should give themselves to God's service with all the power of their will. What an encouragement this should be to us to humbly wait upon God with an upright heart; we may be assured that His eye will be upon us and will show forth His mighty power in us and in our work.

THE OMNIPOTENCE OF GOD

"I am the Almighty God."
Gen. 17:1

When Abraham heard these words, he fell on his face; and God spoke to him. O Christian, have you bowed in deep humility before God until you felt that you were in living contact with the Almighty, until your heart has been filled with the faith that the Almighty God is working in you and will perfect His work in you? Do you wonder that many Christians complain of weakness and shortcomings? They do not understand that the Almighty God must work in them every hour of the day. That is the secret of the true life of faith.

THE FEAR OF GOD

*"Blessed is the man
that feareth the Lord, ..."*
Ps. 112:1

The fear of God – these words characterize the religion of the Old Testament. It is often said that the lack of the fear of God is one thing in which our modern times cannot compare favorably with the time of the Puritans and the Covenanters. No wonder there is much cause of complaint regarding the reading of God's Word, the worship of His House and the absence of that spirit of continuous prayer which marked the early Church.

GOD INCOMPREHENSIBLE

*"Behold, God is great, and
we know Him not, ..."*
Job 36:26

Just think -

His Greatness	Incomprehensible.
His Might	Incomprehensible.
His Omnipresence	Incomprehensible.
His Wisdom	Incomprehensible.
His Holiness	Incomprehensible.
His Mercy	Incomprehensible.
His Love	Incomprehensible.

As we worship, let us cry out: What an inconceivable glory is in this Great Being who is my God and Father!

The Holiness of God (OT)

"Be holy, for I am holy." "I am the Lord, that made you holy."
Lev. 11:45; 19:2; 20:7-8; 21:8,
15, 23; 22:9, 16

Nine times these words are repeated in Leviticus. Israel had to learn that as holiness is the highest and most glorious attribute of God, so it must be the marked characteristic of His people. He that would know God aright and meet Him in secret, must above all desire to be holy as he is holy. The Priests, who were to have access to God, had to be set apart for a life of holiness.

THE HOLINESS OF GOD (NT)

"Holy Father, keep through Thine own name those whom Thou hast given Me. Sanctify them."
John 17:11

Ponder deeply these words as you read them and use them as a prayer to God: "Blessed Lord, strengthen my heart to be unblameable in holiness. God Himself sanctify me wholly. God is faithful, who also will do it." What a privilege to commune with God in secret, to speak these words in prayer, and then to wait upon Him until through the working of the Spirit, they live in our hearts, and we begin to know something of the holiness of God.

Sin

"The chief of sinners." "And the grace of our Lord was exceeding abundant with faith and love which is in Christ Jesus."
1 Tim. 1:14

Never forget for a moment, as you enter the secret chamber, that your whole relation to God depends on what you think of sin and of yourself as a redeemed sinner. It is the thought of sin ever surrounding you and seeking to tempt you, that will keep you low at His feet and give the deep undertone to all your adoration; that will give fervency to your prayer and urgency to the faith that hides itself in Christ.

THE MERCY OF GOD

"Oh, give thanks unto the Lord;
for He is good: for His mercy
endureth forever."
Ps. 136:1

This Psalm is wholly devoted to the praise of God's mercy. In each of the twenty-six verses we have the expression: "His mercy endureth forever." The Psalmist was full of this glad thought. Our hearts too should be filled with the blessed assurance. The everlasting, unchangeable mercy of God is cause for unceasing praise and thanksgiving. Of all God's other attributes, mercy is the crown. May it be a crown upon my head and in my life!

THE WORD OF GOD

*"The Word of God is
quick and powerful."*
Heb. 4:12

The Word teaches me God's will – the will of His promises as to what He will do for me as food for my faith; His commands to which I surrender myself in loving obedience. "God's Word in deepest reverence in our hearts and on our lips and in our lives will be a never-failing fountain of strength and blessing." I believe that God's Word is indeed full of a quickening power that will make me strong. Above all, it will give me the daily blessed fellowship with Thee as the living God.

The Psalms

"How sweet are Thy words unto my taste! yea, sweeter than honey to my mouth!"
Ps. 119:103

Would you each morning truly meet God and worship Him in spirit and in truth, *then let your heart be filled with the Word of God in the Psalms*. As you read the Psalms, underline the word "Lord" or "God", wherever it occurs, and also the pronouns referring to God, "I", "Thou", "He". This will help to connect the contents of the Psalm with God, who is the object of all prayer.

THE GLORY OF GOD

*"Unto Him be glory
throughout all ages."*
Eph. 3:21

What a lesson for the soul that longs to see the glory of God in His Word. Put aside your own efforts and thoughts. Let your heart be as a photographic plate that waits for God's glory to be revealed. The plate must be rightly prepared and clean; let your heart be prepared and purified by God's Spirit. *"Blessed are the pure in heart, for they shall see God."* The plate must be immovable; let your heart be still before God.

THE HOLY TRINITY

"Elect according to ... God the Father ... the Spirit ... and ... Jesus Christ."
1 Peter 1:2

Dear Christian, have you not often felt it a mockery to speak of five minutes to be alone with God, to come under the impression of His glory? And now does not the thought of the true worship of God in Christ through the Holy Spirit make you feel more than ever that it needs time to enter into such holy alliance with God as shall keep the heart and mind all day in His peace and presence? *It is in tarrying in the secret of God's presence that you receive grace to abide in Christ and all the day to be led by His Spirit.*

THE LOVE OF GOD

*"God is love; and he that dwelleth
in love dwelleth in God, and
God in him."*
1 John 4:16

The best and most wonderful word in heaven is Love. For God is Love. And the best and most wonderful word in the inner chamber must be – Love. For the God who meets us there is Love. What is love? The deep desire to give itself for the beloved. Love finds its joy in imparting all that it has to make the loved one happy. And the heavenly Father has no other object than to fill our hearts with His love.

APRIL

WAITING UPON GOD

"On Thee do I wait all the day."
Ps. 25:5

Waiting upon God – in this expression we find one of the deepest truths of God's Word in regard to the attitude of the soul in its communion with God. Just think – that He may reveal Himself in us; teach us all His will; do to us what He has promised; that in all things He may be the Infinite God. The deep root of all Scriptural theology is this: Absolute dependence on God. As we exercise this spirit, it will become more natural and blessedly possible to say: "On thee do I wait all the day."

THE PRAISE OF GOD

"Praise is comely for the upright."
Ps. 33:1

Praise will ever be a part of Adoration. Adoration, when it has entered God's presence and had fellowship with Him, will ever lead to the praise of His name. Let praise be a part of the incense we bring before God in our quiet time. Let us take time to study this until our whole heart and life are one continual song of praise: "I will bless the Lord at all times; His praise shall continually be in my mouth." "Every day will I bless Thee." "I will sing praises unto my God while I have my being."

The Image of God

"And God said, 'Let us make man in our image, after our likeness.'"
Gen. 1:26

Here we have the first thought of man – his origin and his destiny entirely Divine. God undertook the stupendous work of making a creature, who is not God, to be a perfect likeness of Him in His Divine glory. Man was to live in entire dependence on God and to receive directly and unceasingly from Himself the inflow of all that was holy and blessed in the Divine Being. God's glory, His holiness, and His love were to dwell in him and shine out through him.

The Obedience of Faith

"The Lord appeared to Abraham, and said unto him: 'I am God Almighty: walk before Me, and be thou perfect.'"
Gen. 17:1

Children of Abraham, children of God, the Father makes great demands on your faith. If you are to follow in Abraham's footsteps, you too are to forsake all to live in the land of spiritual promise with nothing but His word to depend upon, separated unto God. For this you will need a deep and clear insight that the God who is working in you is the Almighty. Do not think that it is easy to live the life of faith.

The Love of God

"Thou shalt love the Lord thy God with all thine heart, and with all thy soul, and with all thy might."
Deut. 6:5

Let us learn the double lesson. This perfect heart, loving God with all our might, is what God claims, is what God is infinitely worthy of, is what God – blessed be His Name! – *will Himself give and work in us*. Let our whole soul go out in faith to meet, to wait for, and to expect the fulfillment of the promise – to love God with the whole heart is what God Himself will work in us. "The love of God is shed abroad in our hearts by the Holy Spirit given unto us."

THE JOYFUL SOUND

"Blessed is the people that know the joyful sound: ... In Thy name do they rejoice all the day."
Ps. 89:15-16

"Glad tidings of great joy," was what the angel calls the Gospel message. This is what is here spoken of as "the joyful sound." That blessedness consists in God's people walking in the light of God and rejoicing in His name all the day. Undisturbed fellowship, everlasting joy is their portion. Even in the Old Testament such was at times the experience of the saints. But the Old Testament could not secure that. Only the New Testament can and does give it.

THE THOUGHTS OF GOD

*"... so are My thoughts higher
than your thoughts."*
Isa. 55:9

What deep reverence, humility and patience
become us in waiting upon God to impart to us
that which can make us feel at home with the
thoughts in us. What need of daily, tender,
abiding fellowship with God if we are indeed to
enter into His mind and have His thoughts make
their home in us. And what a faith is needed to
believe that God will not only reveal the beauty
and glory of these thoughts, but will so mightily
work in us that their Divine reality and blessing
shall fill our inmost being.

The New Covenant in Jeremiah 31

"I will make a new covenant with the house of Israel."
Jer. 31:31

In the new covenant God's mighty power will be shown in the heart of everyone who believes the promise: *"They shall not depart from Me."* *"It shall be even so as it hath been spoken unto Me."* Bow in deep stillness before God and believe what He says. The measure of our experience of this power of God will ever be in harmony with the law: *"According to your faith be it unto you."*

THE NEW COVENANT IN EZEKIEL

"I will sprinkle clean water upon you, and ye shall be clean; from all your filthiness will I cleanse you. And I will put My Spirit within you, and cause you to walk in My statutes and ye shall keep My judgment."
Ezek. 36:25-27

Just one thing is needed – the faith in an omnipotent God who will by His wonderful power do what He has promised: *"I the Lord have spoken it, and will do it."* Oh, let us begin to believe that the promise will come true. Let us believe all that God here promises.

The New Covenant and Prayer

"Call unto Me, and I will answer thee, and will shew thee great things, and difficult, which thou knowest not."
Jer. 33:3 R.V.

The fulfillment of the great promises of the new covenant is made dependent of prayer. It is when individual men and women turn to God with their whole heart to plead these promises that He will fulfill them. It is in the exercise of intense persevering prayer that faith will be strengthened to take hold of God and surrender itself to His omnipotent working.

THE NEW COVENANT IN HEBREWS

"For I will be merciful to their iniquities, and their sins will I remember no more."
Heb. 8:12

Jesus Christ is "the Mediator of the new covenant," with the forgiveness of sin in the power of His blood and the law written in the heart in the power of His Spirit. Oh that we could understand that just as surely as the complete pardon of sin is assured, the complete fulfillment of the promises may be expected too.

THE TRIAL OF FAITH

> *"'..., if the prophet had bid thee do some great thing, wouldst thou not have done it? How much rather then, when he saith to thee, Wash, and be clean.'"*
> 2 Kings 5:13

In Naaman we have a striking Old Testament illustration of the place faith takes in God's dealing with us. Think first of how intense Naaman's desire was for healing. He would do anything. In this seeking for God and His blessing we have the root of a strong faith which is too much lacking in our religion.

FAITH IN CHRIST

"Ye believe in God, believe also in Me."
John 14:1

Dear Christians, do you not see of what deep importance it is that you take time to worship Jesus in His Divine Omnipotence as one with the Father? That will teach you to count on Him in His sufficiency to work in us all that we can desire. This faith must so possess us that every thought of Christ will be filled with the consciousness of His presence as an Almighty Redeemer, able to save and sanctify and empower us to the very uttermost.

CHRIST'S LIFE IN US

"Because I live, ye shall live also."
John 14:19

Alas, how many there are who are content with the beginnings of the Christian life but never long to have it in its fullness, the more abundant life! They do not believe in it; they are not ready for the sacrifice implied in being wholly filled with the life of Jesus. I pray you, do take time, and let Christ's wonderful promise take possession of your heart. Be content with nothing less than a full salvation, *Christ living in you, and you living in Christ.*

The Obedience of Love

"If ye keep My commandments, ye shall abide in My love."
John 15:10

The question is often asked: How can I come to abide in Christ always? To live wholly for Him? Such is my desire and fervent prayer. In our text the Lord gives the simple but far-reaching answer: "Keep My commandments." This is the only, the sure, the blessed way of abiding in Him. "If ye keep My commandments, ye shall abide in My love; even as I have kept My Father's commandments and abide in His love." Loving obedience is the way to the enjoyment of His love.

THE PROMISE OF THE SPIRIT

"If I go away, the Comforter
will come unto you."
John 16:7

It is this Spirit of God and of Christ that the Church lacks so sadly; it is this Spirit she grieves so unceasingly. It is owing to this that her work is so often feeble and fruitless. And what can be the reason of this? The Spirit is God. He claims as God to have possession of our whole being. We have thought too much of Him as our help in the Christian life; we have not known that heart and life are to be entirely and unceasingly under His control; we are to be led by the Spirit every day and every hour.

In Christ

*"In that day ye shall know that
I am in My Father, and ye in
Me, and I in you."*
John 14:20

Blessed Lord, we beseech Thee, teach us to surrender ourselves unreservedly to the Holy Spirit and so daily above everything to wait for His teaching, that we too may know the blessed secret, that *as Thou art in the Father and the Father worketh through Thee, so we are in Thee, and Thou workest through us.*

Abiding in Christ

"Abide in Me, and I in you."
John 15:4

The great need is to take time in waiting on the Lord Jesus in the power of His Spirit, until the two great truths get the complete mastery of your being. As Christ is in God – this is the testimony from heaven; as the branch is in the vine – this is the testimony of all nature. The law of heaven and the law of earth combine in calling us: "Abide in Christ." "He that abideth in Me, bringeth forth much fruit." Fruit, more fruit, much fruit is what Christ seeks, is what He works, is what He will assuredly give to the soul that trusts Him.

THE POWER OF PRAYER

*"... ask whatsoever ye will, and it
shall be done unto you."*
John 15:7 R.V.

Before our Lord went to heaven He taught His
disciples two great lessons in regard to their
relation to Him in the great work they had to do.
The one was that in Heaven He would have much
more power than He had upon earth and that He
would use that power for the salvation of men,
solely through them, their word and their work.
The other was that they without Him could do
nothing, but that they could count upon Him to
work in them and through them and so carry out
His purpose.

The Mystery of Love

*"I pray that they may all be one;
even as Thou, Father, art in Me,
and I in Thee ..."*
John 17:21

The power to convince the world that God loved the disciples as He loved His Son could only come as believers lived out their life of having Christ in them and proving it by loving their brethren as Christ loved them. The feebleness of the Church is owing to this – that our life in Christ and His life in us is not known and not proved to the world by the living unity in which our love manifests that Christ is in us.

CHRIST OUR RIGHTEOUSNESS

*"Justified freely by His grace
through the redemption that
is in Christ Jesus."*
Rom. 3:24

Justification comes at the commencement full and complete, as the eye of faith is fixed upon Christ. But that is only the beginning. Gradually believers begin to understand that they were at the same time born again, *that they have Christ in them, and that their calling now is to abide in Christ, and let Christ abide and live and work in them.* The grace of pardon is but the beginning; growing in grace leads on to fuller insight.

CHRIST OUR LIFE

*"Reckon ye also yourselves to be
dead unto sin, but alive unto
God in Christ Jesus."*
Rom. 6:11 R.V.

In very deed, just as the new life in us is an actual participation in and experience of the risen life of Christ, so our death to sin in Christ is also an actual spiritual reality. It is when, by the power of the Holy Spirit, we are enabled to see how really we were one with Christ on the cross in His death and in His resurrection, that we shall understand that in Him sin has no power over us. We present ourselves unto God "as alive from the dead".

CRUCIFIED WITH CHRIST

"I have been crucified with Christ;
yet I live; and yet no longer I, but
Christ liveth in me."
Gal. 2:20

As in Adam we died out of the life and the will of God into sin and corruption, so in Christ we are made partakers of a new spiritual death, a death to sin and into the will and the life of God. Such was the death Christ died; such is the death we are made partakers of in Him. To Paul this was such a reality that he was able to say: "I have been crucified with Christ ..." This death had such power that he no longer lived his own life; Christ lived His life in him.

THE FAITH LIFE

"That life which I now live in the flesh, I live in faith, the faith which is in the Son of God, who loved me and gave Himself up for me."
Gal. 2:20 R.V.

If we ask Paul what he meant by saying that he no longer lives but that Christ lives in him, what now is his part in living that life? He gives us the answer: His whole life, day by day and all the day, was an unceasing faith in the wonderful love that had given itself for him. Faith was the power that possessed and permeated his whole being and his every action.

Full Consecration

*"Yea, verily, and I count all
things to be loss for the excellency of the knowledge of
Christ Jesus my Lord."*
Phil. 3:8

But how little the Church understands that we
have been entirely redeemed from the world, to
live wholly and only for God and His love. Christ
claims the whole heart and the whole life and the
whole strength, if we are indeed to share with
Him in the victory through the power of the Holy
Spirit. The law of the kingdom is unchangeable
– *all things loss for the excellency of the
knowledge of Christ Jesus my Lord.*

Entire Sanctification

*"And the God of peace Himself
sanctify you wholly; and may your
spirit and soul and body be preserved entire, without blame at the
coming of our Lord Jesus Christ.
Faithful is He that calleth you,
who will also do it."*
1 Thess. 5:23-24 R.V.

What a promise! One would expect to see all
God's children clinging to it, claiming its fulfillment. Alas, unbelief does not know what to
think of it, and but few count it their treasure and
joy. Just listen. God, the God of peace – keeping
our hearts and thoughts in Christ Jesus – none
other but Himself can and will do it.

THE EXCEEDING GREATNESS OF HIS POWER

"... that the God of our Lord Jesus Christ, ... give unto you a spirit of wisdom and revelation; ... that ye may know what is the exceeding greatness of His power to us-ward who believe, ..."
Eph. 1:17-19 R.V.

It is by that Almighty power that the risen and exalted Christ can be revealed in our hearts as our life and our strength. Oh, let us cry to God, let us trust God for His Holy Spirit to enable us to claim nothing less every day that the exceeding greatness of this resurrection power.

THE INDWELLING CHRIST

"That Christ may dwell in your heart by faith."
Eph. 3:14-19

The great privilege that separated Israel from other nations was this: they had God dwelling in their midst, His Home in the Holiest of all, in the tabernacle and the temple. The New Testament is the dispensation of the indwelling God in the Heart of His people. The Gospel – the dispensation of the indwelling Christ. How few Christians there are who believe or experience it!

CHRISTIAN PERFECTION

*"The God of peace make you
perfect in every good work to do
His will, working in you that which
is well-pleasing in His sight,
through Jesus Christ."*
Heb. 13:20-21

The great thought here is that all that Christ
had wrought out for our redemption and all
that God had done in raising Him from the
dead was just with the one object that He might
now have free scope for working out in us that
everlasting redemption which Christ had
brought in. He Himself as God the Omnipotent
will make us perfect in every good work.

THE GOD OF ALL GRACE

*"The God of all grace, who called
you unto His eternal glory in Christ,
shall Himself perfect, stablish,
strengthen you, after ye have
suffered a little while."*
1 Peter 5:10

Just as God is the centre of the universe, the one source of its strength, the one Guide that orders and controls its movements, so God must have the same place in the life of the believer. With every new day the first and chief thought ought to be – God, God alone, can fit me this day to live as He would have me.

MAY

NOT SINNING

*"Ye know that He was manifested
to take away sins; and in Him is
no sin. Whosoever abideth in
Him sinneth not."*
1 John 3:5-6

In our text John teaches how we can be kept from sinning: "He that abideth in Christ sinneth not." Though there is sin in our nature, the abiding in Christ, in whom is no sin, does indeed free us from the power of sin and enables us day by day to live so as to please God.

Overcoming the World

"Who is he that overcometh the world, but he that believeth that Jesus is the Son of God."
1 John 5:5

The world still exerts a terrible influence over the Christian who does not know that in Christ he has been crucified to the world. In the pleasure in eating and drinking, in the love and enjoyment of what there is to be seen of its glory, and in all that constitutes the pride of life, the power of this world proves itself. And most Christians are either utterly ignorant of the danger of a worldly spirit or feel themselves utterly powerless to conquer it.

JESUS: THE AUTHOR AND PERFECTOR OF OUR FAITH

"Lord, I believe; help Thou mine unbelief."
Mark 9:24

What a lesson for us who have so often felt that our faith was too feeble to grasp the precious gift. And here we receive the assurance that the Christ is a Savior *who Himself will care for our faith*. Even though it be but as a mustard seed; in contact with Christ the feeblest faith is made strong and bold. Jesus Christ is the Author and Perfector of our faith.

THE LOST SECRET

" ... ye shall be baptized with the Holy Spirit not many days hence."
Acts 1:5

The Church appears to have lost possession of that which ought to be to her a secret of secrets – the abiding consciousness, day by day, that it is only as she lives in the power of the Holy Spirit that she can preach the Gospel in demonstration of the Spirit and of power. It is owing to this that there is so much preaching and working with so little of spiritual result, and especially that there is so little of that much-availing prayer that brings down the Power from on high on her ministrations.

THE KINGDOM OF GOD

"Jesus showed Himself to His disciples ... speaking of the things pertaining to the Kingdom of God."
Acts 1:3

In the last command our Lord gave to His disciples (Acts 1:4, 8) we shall find the great essential characteristics of the Kingdom put in great power. 1. The King – the crucified Christ. 2. The disciples – His faithful followers. 3. The power for their service – the Holy Spirit. 4. Their work – testifying for Christ as His witnesses. 5. Their aim – the ends of the earth. 6. Their first duty – waiting on God in united, unceasing prayer.

CHRIST AS KING

*"'... there be some of them which
stand here, which shall not taste
of death, till they have seen the
Kingdom of God.'"*
Mark 9:1

This must be our first lesson if we are to follow in the steps of the disciples and to share their blessing, that we must know that Christ actually as King dwells and rules in our hearts. We must know that we live in Him and in His power are able to accomplish all that He would have us do. Our whole life is to be devoted to our King and the service of His Kingdom.

JESUS THE CRUCIFIED

*"God hath made that same Jesus,
whom ye have crucified,
both Lord and Christ."*
Acts 2:36

Each one of us needs to experience this fellowship with Christ in His cross if the Spirit of Pentecost is really to take possession of us. It is as we become "conformable to His death", in the entire surrender of our will, in the entire self-denial of our old nature, in the entire separation from the spirit of this world, that we can become the worthy servants of a crucified King, and our hearts the worthy temples of His glory.

THE APOSTLES

"He charged them ... to wait for the promise of the Father."
Acts 1:4 R.V.

Let this be the test by which we try ourselves whether we have indeed surrendered to the fellowship of Christ's sufferings and death, hated our own life and crucified it – and received the power of Christ's life in us. This will give us liberty to believe that God will hear our prayer too and give us His Holy Spirit to work in us what we and He desire, if we are indeed with one accord to take up the disciples' prayer and to share in the answer.

NOT OF THIS WORLD

*"They are not of the world even
as I am not of the world."*
John 17:14, 16

One great mark of the disciples was thus to
be that as little as Christ was of the world, so
little were they to be of the world. Christ and
they had become united in the cross and the
resurrection; they both belonged to another
world, the Kingdom of heaven. This separation
from the world is to be the mark of all disciples
who long to be filled with the Spirit.

OBEDIENCE

"If ye love Me, ye will keep my commandments ... and He shall give you another Comforter."
John 14:15-16

Is Christ something or nothing or everything to us? For the unconverted, Christ is nothing; for the half converted – the average Christian – Christ is something; for the true Christian, Christ is all. Each one who prays for the power of the Spirit must be ready to say: "I yield myself with my whole heart this day to the leading of the Spirit"; a full surrender is the question of life or death, an absolute necessity.

THE HOLY SPIRIT

*"Ye shall receive power when the
Holy Spirit is come upon you."*
Acts 1:8

The Spirit now reveals Christ in us as first of
all our life and then our strength for a perfect
obedience and the preaching of the Word in
the power of God. Amazing mystery! The Spirit
of God, our life; the Spirit of Christ, our light
and strength. It is as men and women who are
led by this Spirit of the first disciples, that we
shall have the power to pray the effectual prayer
of the righteous that availeth much.

The Power from on High

*"Tarry ye until ye be clothed
with power from on high."*
Luke 24:49

The Holy Spirit would not be a power in them which they could possess. But He would possess them, and their work would be in very deed the work of the Almighty Christ. Their whole posture each day would be that of unceasing dependence, prayer and confident expectation. Everything calls the Gospel minister to rest content with nothing less than the indwelling life and power of the Holy Spirit revealing Jesus in the heart as the only fitness for preaching the Gospel in power.

MY WITNESSES

"Ye shall be My Witnesses."
Acts 1:8

This is the only weapon that the King allows His redeemed ones to use. Without claiming authority or power, without wisdom or eloquence, without influence or position, each one is called, not only by his words but by his life and action, to be a living *proof and witness of what Jesus can do.* Here we have the secret of a flourishing Church: *every believer a witness for Jesus.* Here we have the cause of the weakness of the Church: so few who are willing in daily life to testify that Jesus is Lord.

THE GOSPEL MINISTRY

*"The Spirit of truth, He
shall testify of Me, and ye
shall also bear witness ..."*
John 15:26-27

My witnesses – that not only refers to all believers, but very especially to all ministers of the Gospel. This is the high calling and also the only power of the preacher of the Gospel – in everything to be *a witness for Jesus*. He may never forget that it is for this especially that he has been set apart, to be with the Holy Spirit a witness for Christ. It is as he does this that sinners will find salvation, that God's children will be sanctified and fitted for His service.

THE WHOLE WORLD

*"My witnesses unto the utter-
most parts of the earth."*
Acts 1:8

Oh, that Christian people might understand that the extension of God's Kingdom can only be effected by the united continued prayer of men and women who give their hearts wholly to wait upon Christ in the assurance that what they desire He will do for them. Oh, that God would grant that His children proved their faith in Christ by making His aim their aim and yielding themselves to be His witnesses in united, persevering prayer.

The Whole Earth Filled with His Glory

*"... let the whole earth
be filled with His glory ..."*
Ps. 72:19

What a prospect! This earth now under the power of the Evil One renewed and *filled with the glory of God* – a new earth wherein righteousness dwells. Though we believe it so little, it will surely come to pass; God's Word is the pledge of it. God's Son by His blood and death conquered the power of sin, and through the Eternal Spirit the power of God is working out His purpose.

The First Prayer Meeting

*"These all with one accord
continued steadfastly in prayer,
with the women."*
Acts 1:14

It is difficult to form a right conception of the unspeakable importance of this first prayer meeting in the history of the Kingdom, a prayer meeting which was the simple fulfilling of the command of Christ. It was to be for all time the indication of the one condition on which His Presence and Spirit would be known in Power. In it we have the secret key that opens the storehouse of heaven with all its blessings.

THE UNITY OF THE SPIRIT

"Endeavoring to keep the unity of the Spirit. There is one body and one Spirit."
Eph. 4:3-4

Let none of us think it too much to give a quarter of an hour every day for meditation on some word of God connected with His promises to His Church – and then to plead with Him for its fulfillment. Slowly, unobservedly, and yet surely, you will taste the blessedness of being one, heart and soul, with God's people and receive the power to pray the effectual prayer that availeth much.

Union Is Strength

"And when they had prayed, they were all filled with the Holy Spirit, and they spoke the Word of God with boldness. And the multitude of them that believed were of one heart and one soul."
Acts 4:31-32

The power of union we see everywhere in nature. How feeble is a drop of rain, but many drops united in one stream, thus becoming one body, is an irresistible power. Such is the power of true union in prayer. Such was the prayer in the upper room. And such can our prayer be if we unite all our forces.

PRAYER IN THE NAME OF CHRIST

*"Whatsoever ye shall ask in
My Name, that will I do, ..."*
John 14:13

If the thought comes to us that such prayer is not easy of attainment, we only need to remember what Christ told them. *It was when the Holy Spirit came that they would have power thus to pray.* It is to draw us on to yield ourselves fully to the control of the blessed Spirit that He holds out to us the precious promise, "Ask and ye shall receive, that your joy may be full." As we believe in the power of the Spirit working in us in full measure, intercession will become to us the joy and the strength of all our service.

YOUR HEAVENLY FATHER

"Our Father which art in heaven."
Luke 11:2

We count it a great privilege as we bow in worship to know that the Father comes near to us where we are upon earth. But we soon begin to feel the need of rising up to enter into His Holy Presence in heaven, to breathe its atmosphere, to drink in its spirit, and to become truly heavenly-minded. And as we in the power of thought and imagination leave earth behind, and in the power of the Holy Spirit enter the Holiest of all where the seraphs worship, the word "heavenly Father" gets a new meaning.

THE POWER OF PRAYER

"The effectual fervent prayer of a righteous man availeth much."
James 5:16

"The *effectual fervent prayer* of a righteous man availeth much." It is only when the righteous man stirs up himself and rouses his whole being to take hold of God that the prayer availeth much. As Jacob said: "I will not let thee go"; as the importunate widow gave the just Judge no rest, so it is that the effectual fervent prayer effects great things.

PRAYER AND SACRIFICE

"I would that ye knew what great conflict I have for you."
Col. 2:1

Prayer is sacrifice. Our prayer has its worth alone from being rooted in the sacrifice of Jesus Christ. Need we wonder at the lack of power in our prayer where there is so much reluctance to make the needful sacrifice in waiting upon God. Christ, the Christ we trust in, The Christ that lives in us offered Himself a sacrifice to God. It is as this spirit lives and rules in us that we shall receive power from Him as intercessors to pray the effectual prayer that availeth much.

THE INTERCESSION OF THE SPIRIT FOR THE SAINTS

"... He maketh intercession for the saints according to the Will of God."
Rom. 8:27

Where and how does the Spirit make intercession for the saints? In no other way than that, in the heart which knows not what to pray, He secretly and effectually prays what is according to the Will of God. This of course implies that we trust Him to do His work in us and that we tarry before God even when we know what to pray, in the assurance that the Holy Spirit is praying in us.

THAT THEY ALL MAY BE ONE

*"Holy Father, keep them in
Thy Name ... that they may be
one, even as we are ..."*
John 17:11

How little the church has understood this. How little its different branches are marked by a fervent affectionate love to all the saints of whatever name or denomination. Shall we not welcome heartily the prayer *"that they may be one"* a chief part of our daily fellowship with God? How simple it would be when once we connected the two words "Our Father," with all the children of God throughout the world.

THE DISCIPLES' PRAYER

*"They continued steadfastly in
fellowship and in prayers."*
Acts 2:42

Just think of the object of their desire. However defective the thoughts were that they had of the Blessed Spirit, this they knew, from the words of Jesus, "it is expedient for you that I go away," that the Spirit would give the glorified Christ into their very hearts in a way they had never known Him before. And it would be He Himself, in the mighty power of God's Spirit, who would be their strength for the work to which He had called them.

PAUL'S CALL TO PRAYER

*"... praying at all
seasons in the Spirit ..."*
Eph. 6:18 R.V.

He expects believers to be so filled with the consciousness of their being in Christ and through Him united consciously to the whole body, that in their daily life and all its engagements, their highest aim would ever be the welfare of the body of Christ of which they had become members. Is not this what we need in our daily life, that every believer who is yielded undividedly to Christ Jesus shall live in the consciousness of oneness with Christ and His body?

PAUL'S REQUEST FOR PRAYER

*"... that I may open my mouth boldly,
to make known the mystery of the
Gospel, that therein I may speak
boldly, as I ought to speak."*
Eph. 6:19-20

Paul had now been a minister of the Gospel for more than twenty years. One would say that it would come naturally to him to speak boldly. But so deep is his conviction of his own insufficiency and weakness, so absolute is his dependence on Divine teaching and power, that he feels that without the direct help of God he cannot do the work as it ought to be done.

Prayer for All Saints

*"To the Saints and faithful brethren
in Christ, ... We give thanks to
God, praying always for you, ..."*
Col. 1:1-4

Prayer for all saints: let this be our first thought. It will need time and thought and love to realize what is included in that simple expression. Think of your own neighborhood and the saints you know; of your whole country and praise God for all who are His saints; of all Christian nations of the world and the saints to be found in each of these; of all the heathen nations and the saints of God to be found among them in ever-increasing numbers.

PRAYER BY ALL SAINTS

*"We trust in God that He will yet
deliver us; you also helping together by prayer for us."*
2 Cor. 1:10-11

If we are to ask God to increase the number and
the power of those who do pray, we shall be led
to form some impression of what the hope is
that our circle of intercessors may gradually
increase in number and power. It may be that
in time believers will stand together in small
circles, or throughout wider districts, in helping to rouse those around them to take heart in
the great work that the prayer *for all saints* may
become *one by all saints*.

Prayer for All the Fullness of the Spirit

"... and prove me now there with, saith the Lord of Hosts, if I will not ... pour you out a blessing that there shall not be room enough to receive it."
Mal. 3:10

What a cry of need there is throughout the whole Church and all our mission fields. The only remedy for inefficiency or weakness to enable us to gain the victory over the powers of this world or of darkness is in the manifested presence of our Lord in the midst of His hosts and in the power of His Spirit.

JUNE

Every Day

*"Give us day by day
our daily bread."*
Luke 11:3

There are some Christians who are afraid of the thoughts of a promise to pray every day as altogether beyond them. They could not undertake it, and yet they pray to God to give them their bread day by day. Surely if the children of God themselves once yielded themselves with their whole lives to God's love and service, they should count it a privilege to avail themselves of any invitation that would help them *every day* to come into God's Presence with the great need of His Church and Kingdom.

WITH ONE ACCORD

"They were all with one accord in one place ... and they were all filled with the Holy Spirit."
Acts 2:1, 4

The strength unity gives is something inconceivable. The power of each individual member is increased to a large degree by the inspiration of fellowship with a large and conquering host. Nothing can so help us to an ever-larger faith as the consciousness of being one body and one spirit in Christ Jesus. It was as the disciples were all with one accord in one place in the Day of Pentecost that they were all filled with the Holy Spirit.

A Personal Call

*"We trust not in ourselves, but in
God who delivered us, and will yet
deliver us."*
2 Cor. 1:9-10

Texts like these prove that there were still
Christians in the churches under the full power
of the Holy Spirit on whom Paul could count
for effectual, much-availing prayer. When we
plead with Christians to pray without ceasing,
there are a very large number who quietly
decide that such a life is not possible for them.
And yet it is to such that we bring the call to offer
ourselves for a whole-hearted surrender to
live entirely for Christ.

The Redemption of the Cross

"Christ redeemed us ..."
Gal. 3:13

The preaching of the redemption of the cross is the foundation and center of the salvation the Gospel brings us. To those who believe its full truth, it is a cause of unceasing thanksgiving. It gives us boldness to rejoice in God. There is nothing which will keep the heart more tender toward God, enabling us to live in His love and make Him known to those who have never yet found Him. God be praised for the redemption of the cross.

THE FELLOWSHIP OF THE CROSS

"Have this mind in you, which was also in Christ Jesus."
Phil. 2:5

Paul here tells us what that mind was in Christ: He emptied Himself; He took the form of a servant; He humbled Himself, even to the death of the cross. It is this mind that was in Christ, the deep humility that gave up His life to the very death, that is to be the spirit that animates us. It is thus that we shall prove and enjoy the blessed fellowship of His cross.

CRUCIFIED WITH CHRIST

*"I have been crucified with Christ;
yet I live; and yet no longer I, but
Christ liveth in me."*
Gal. 2:20

The thought of fellowship with Christ in His bearing the cross has often led to the vain attempt in our own power to follow Him and bear His image. But this is impossible until we know the meaning of, "I have been crucified with Christ." As faith realizes that I no longer live but Christ lives in me as the Crucified one, life in the fellowship of the cross becomes a possibility and a blessed experience.

CRUCIFIED TO THE WORLD

*"Far be it from me to glory, save in
the cross of our Lord Jesus Christ,
through which the world hath been
crucified unto me, and I unto the
world."*
Gal. 6:14

O Christian, when the world crucified Christ,
it crucified you with Him. When Christ overcame the world on the cross, He made you an
overcomer too. He calls you now, at whatever
cost of self-denial, to regard the world in its
hostility to God and His Kingdom as a crucified
enemy over whom the cross can ever keep you
conqueror.

JUNE 8

The Flesh Crucified

*"They that are in Christ Jesus have
crucified the flesh with the passions
and the lusts thereof."*
Gal. 5:24

Alas, how many there are who have never for
a moment thought of such a thing! It may be
that the preaching of Christ crucified has been
defective. It may be that the truth of our being
crucified with Christ has not been taught. They
shrink back from the self-denial that it implies,
and as a result, where the flesh is allowed in
any measure to have its way, the Spirit of
Christ cannot exert His power.

BEARING THE CROSS

"He that doth not take his cross and follow after Me, is not worthy of Me. He that loseth his life for My sake shall find it."
Matt. 10:38-39

The disciples had often seen an evil-doer bearing his cross to the place of execution. In bearing the cross, he acknowledged the sentence of death that was on him. And Christ would have His disciples understand that their nature was so evil and corrupt that it was only in losing their natural life that they could find the true life.

SELF—DENIAL

"Then said Jesus unto His disciples, 'If any man will come after Me, let him deny himself, and take up his cross, and follow Me.'"
Matt. 16:24

Death to self is to be the Christian's watchword. The surrender to Christ is to be so entire, the surrender for Christ's sake to live for those around us so complete, that self is never allowed to come down from the cross to which it has been crucified but is ever kept in the place of death.

HE CANNOT BE MY DISCIPLE

*"If any man cometh unto Me,
and hateth not his own life, he
cannot be My disciple."*
Luke 14:26

Christ claims all. Christ undertakes to satisfy every need and to give a hundredfold more than we give up. It is when by faith we become conscious what it means to know Christ and to love Him and to receive from Him what can in very deed enrich and satisfy our immortal spirits, that we shall count the surrender of what at first appeared so difficult, our highest privilege.

FOLLOW ME

*"... go thy way, sell whatsoever thou
hast, and come, take up the cross,
and follow Me."*
Mark 10:21

Christ had spoken about bearing the cross
from the human side as the one condition of
discipleship. Here with the rich young ruler He
reveals from the side of God what is needed to
give men the will and the power thus to sacrifice all, if they were to enter the Kingdom. It is
only by Divine power that a man can take up his
cross, can lose his life, can deny himself and
hate the life to which he is by nature so attached.

A Grain of Wheat

*"Verily, verily, I say unto you,
Except a grain of wheat fall into the
earth and die, it abideth by itself
alone; but if it die, it beareth much
fruit. He that loveth his life loseth it;
and he that hateth his life in this
world shall keep it unto life eternal."*
John 12:24-25 R.V.

All nature is the parable of how the losing of a life can be the way of securing a truer and a higher life. Every grain of wheat, every seed throughout the world, teaches the lesson that through death lies the path to beautiful and fruitful life.

Thy Will Be Done

"O My Father, if it be possible, let this cup pass away from Me: nevertheless, not as I will but as Thou wilt."
Matt. 26:39 R.V.

It is from Christ alone that we can learn what it means to have fellowship with His sufferings and to be made conformable unto His death. "Thy will be done"; let this be the deepest and highest word in thy life. In the power of Christ with whom thou hast been crucified and in the power of His Spirit, the daily surrender to the ever-blessed will of God will become the joy and the strength of thy life.

The Love of the Cross

*"Then said Jesus: 'Father,
forgive them; for they know
not what they do.'"*
Luke 23:34

He prays for His enemies. In the hour of their
triumph over Him and of the shame and suffering which they delight in showering on Him,
He pours out His love in prayer for them. It is
the call to everyone who believes in a crucified
Christ to go and do likewise, even as He has
said, "Love your enemies, bless them that
curse you, Do good to them that hate you, and
pray for them which Persecute you."

THE SACRIFICE OF THE CROSS

*"My God, My God, why hast Thou
forsaken Me?"*
Matt. 27:46

How deep must have been the darkness that
overshadowed Him, when not one ray of light
could pierce and He could not say, "My Father"! It was this awful desertion that caused
Him the agony and the bloody sweat in
Gethsemane. It was His love to God and love to
man, yielding Himself to the very uttermost. It
is as we learn to believe and to worship that
love, that we too shall learn to say: "Abba,
Father, Thy will be done."

The Death of the Cross

*"'Father, into Thy hands I commit
My spirit.'"*
Luke 23:46

Like David (Ps. 31:5), Christ had often committed His spirit into the hands of His Father for His daily life and need. But here is something new and very special. He gives up His spirit into the power of death, gives up all control over it, to sink down into the darkness and death of the grave where he can neither think nor pray, nor will. He surrenders Himself to the utmost into the Father's hands, trusting Him to care for Him in the dark and in due time to raise Him up again.

It Is Finished

"When Jesus had received the vinegar, He said: 'It is finished.'"
John 19:30

With that word He uttered the truth of the gospel of our redemption, that all that was needed for man's salvation had been accomplished on the cross. This disposition should characterize every follower of Christ. The mind that was in Him must be in us – it must be our meat, the strength of our life, *to do the Will of God in all things and to finish His work*. There may be small things about which we are not conscientious and so we bring harm to ourselves and to God's work.

DEAD TO SIN

*"We who died to sin, how shall we
any longer live therein?"*
Rom. 6:2

In these words we have the deep spiritual truth
that our death to sin in Christ delivers us from
its power so that we no longer may or need to
live in it. The secret of true and full holiness is
by faith and in the power of the Holy Spirit to
live in the consciousness I am dead to sin. As
we grow in the consciousness of our union with
the crucified Christ, we shall experience that the
power of His life in us has made us free from the
power of sin.

The Righteousness of God

"Abraham believed God, and it was counted unto him for righteousness." "He believed God, who quickeneth the dead."
Rom. 4:3, 17

Abraham had not only believed this, but something more. There are two essential needs in the redemption of man in Christ Jesus: the need of justification by faith, to restore man to the favor of God. But there is more needed. He must also be quickened to a new life. Just as justification is by faith alone, so is regeneration also. Christ died for our sins; He was raised again out of or through our justification.

DEAD WITH CHRIST

"If we died with Christ, we believe that we shall also live with Him."
Rom. 6:8

The word gives us a Divine assurance of what we actually are and have in Christ. And this is not a truth that our minds can master and appropriate, but a reality which the Holy Spirit will reveal within us. In His power we accept our death with Christ on the cross as the power of our daily life. Everything depends upon our acceptance of the Divine assurance: if we died with Christ as He died and now lives to God, we too have the assurance that in Him we have the power to live unto God.

DEAD TO THE LAW

"Ye were made dead to the law, through the body of Christ." "Having died to that wherein we were holden, so that we serve in newness of the spirit."
Rom. 7:4, 6

The believer is not only dead to sin but dead to the law. This is a deeper truth, giving us deliverance from the thought of a life of effort and failure and opening the way to the life in the power of the Holy Spirit. "Thou shalt" is done away with; the power of the Spirit takes its place. In the latter we have the man who knows that he is in Christ Jesus, dead to sin and alive to God.

THE FLESH CONDEMNED ON THE CROSS

"... God, sending His own Son in the likeness of sinful flesh, and for sin, condemned sin in the flesh."
Rom. 8:3

In me, that is in my flesh, in the old nature which I have from Adam, there dwells literally no good thing that can satisfy the eye of a holy God! And that flesh can never by any process of discipline, or struggling, or prayer, be made better than it is! But the Son of god in the likeness of sinful flesh – in the form of a man – condemned sin on the cross.

JESUS CHRIST AND HIM CRUCIFIED

*"... Jesus Christ and Him crucified.
And my preaching was in demonstration of the Spirit and of power."*
1 Cor. 2:2, 4

Have we not here the great reason why the power of God is so little manifested in the preaching of the Gospel? Christ the crucified may be the subject of the preaching and yet there may be such confidence in human learning and eloquence that there is nothing to be seen of that likeness of the crucified Jesus which alone gives preaching its supernatural, its divine power.

LOOKING UNTO JESUS

"Let us run with patience the race that is set before us, looking unto Jesus, the Author and Perfector of our faith, who for the joy that was set before Him endured the cross, ..."
Heb. 12:1-2 R.V.

It was for the joy set before Him that Christ endured the cross – the joy of pleasing and glorifying the Father, of loving and winning souls for Himself. As Christ found His highest happiness through His endurance of the cross, so it is only *in our fellowship of the cross* that we can really become conformed to the image of God's Son.

Without the Gate

"Wherefore Jesus also, that He might sanctify the people through His own blood, suffered without the gate. Let us go forth therefore unto Him without the camp, bearing His reproach."
Heb. 13:12-13

There are many Christians who love to hear of the boldness with which we can enter into the Holy Place through His blood, who yet have little desire for the fellowship of His reproach and are unwilling to separate themselves from the world with the same boldness with which they think to enter the sanctuary.

JULY

Alive unto Righteousness

"Who His own self bare our sins in His own body on the tree, that we, having died unto sins, might live unto righteousness."
1 Peter 2:24 R.V.

It means that we realize by faith how actually we shared with Christ in His death and now, as He lives in us, abide in unceasing fellowship with Him, the Crucified One. This costs self-sacrifice; it costs earnest prayer; it costs a whole-hearted surrender to God and His will and the cross of Jesus; it costs abiding in Christ and unceasing fellowship with Him.

FOLLOWERS OF THE CROSS

*"Hereby know we love, because
He laid down His life for us: and
we ought to lay down our lives
for the brethren."*
1 John 3:16 R.V.

It is only as the great truth of the indwelling Christ obtains a place in the faith of the Church which it has not now, that the Christ-like love to one another will become the mark of true Christianity by which the world shall know that we are Christ's disciples. This is what will bring the world to believe that God has loved us even as He loved Christ.

Following the Lamb

*"These are they which follow the
Lamb whithersoever He goeth."*
Rev. 14:4

Children of God oh, come and study the Lamb
who is to be your model and your Savior. Let
Paul's words be the keynote of your life: "I have
been crucified with Christ; yet I live; and yet no
longer I, but Christ liveth in me." Here you
have the way to follow the Lamb even to the
glory of the Throne of God in Heaven.

TO HIM BE THE GLORY

"Unto Him that loved us, and washed us from our sins in His own blood, and hath made us kings and priests unto God and His Father; to Him be glory and dominion forever and ever: Amen."

Rev. 1:5-6

Love makes everything easy. Do not think of your love to Him but of His great love to you, given through the Holy Spirit. Meditate on this day and night until you have the assurance: He loves me unspeakably. It is through the love of Christ on the cross that souls are drawn to Him.

The Blessing of the Cross

"But God forbid that I should glory, save in the cross of our Lord Jesus Christ, by whom the world is crucified into me, and I unto the world."
Gal. 6:14

One of the blessings of the cross consists in this, that it teaches us to know the worthlessness of our efforts and the utter corruption of our own nature. The cross does not offer to improve human nature or to supply what we are unable to do. Many people, indeed, use it in this way, like patching a new cloth on an old garment.

JULY 6

THE ABIDING PRESENCE

"Lo, I am with you alway, even unto the end of the world."
Matt. 28:20

In all the work of the minister and the missionary, everything depends on the consciousness, through a living faith, of the abiding presence of the Lord with His servant, the living experience of the presence of Jesus as an essential element in preaching the Gospel. If this is clouded, work becomes a human effort without the freshness and the power of the heavenly life.

THE OMNIPOTENCE OF CHRIST

"All power is given unto Me in heaven and on earth."
Matt. 28:18

Let us remember that this power is never meant to be experienced as if it were our own. It is only as Jesus Christ as a living Person dwells and works with His divine energy in our own heart and life that there can be power in our preaching as a personal testimony.

The Omnipresence of Christ

"Certainly I will be with thee."
Ex. 3:12

The revelation of God's omnipresence in the man Christ Jesus makes the grace that enables us to claim this presence as our strength and our joy something inexpressibly blessed. And yet how many a servant of Christ, when the promise is given, finds it difficult to understand all that is implied in it and how it can become the practical experience of daily life.

CHRIST: THE SAVIOR OF THE WORLD

*"This is indeed the Christ,
the Savior of the world."*
John 4:42

It is only when His servants in their lives show that they obey Him in all His commands, that they can expect the fullness of His power and His presence to be with them. The abiding presence of the Savior from sin is promised to all who have accepted Him in the fullness of His redeeming power and who preach by their lives as well as by their words what a wonderful Savior He is.